SOU TAILGATING

Game Day Recipes and Traditions

To Blair, Michael, and Will

SOUTHERN TAILGATING

Game Day Recipes and Traditions

by Michael Dean Looney
and Kimberly Looney

VISION PRESS   P.O. Box 1106   Northport, AL 35476

The authors

Dean Looney is a graduate of the University of Georgia, and Kim graduated from Valdosta (Ga.) State College. She is a kindergarten teacher, and Dean a newspaper journalist.

On the cover

Kay Arnold (serving), Kecia Arnold, Ed Howell, and Earline Howell enjoy fellowship and a well-prepared meal before an Alabama-Vanderbilt game. (Photograph by Amy Kilpatrick)

Vision Press
3230 Mystic Lake Way
P.O. Box 1106
Northport, Alabama 35476

Library of Congress Cataloguing-in-Publication Data

Looney, Michael D., 1963-
      Southern tailgating : game day recipes and traditions / Michael D. Looney, Kimberly S. Looney.
            p.   cm.
      ISBN 0-9630700-9-6
      1. Outdoor cookery. 2. Picnicking. 3. Cookery, American--Southern style.   I. Looney, Kimberly S., 1964-   . II. Title.
TX823.L66 1994
641.5'78---dc20   94-23210
                                                                          CIP

Printed in the United States of America

In the East, college football is a cultural exercise. On the West Coast, it is a tourist attraction. In the Midwest, it is cannibalism. But in the South it is religion, and Saturday is the holy day.

Marino Casem
Alcorn State University

We got off of this truck and followed this little bunch of people through this small, little bitty patch of woods, thar. It says, "Get somethin' to eat here." And I went up and got two hotdogs and a Big Orange drink.

Andy Griffith
"What It Was Was Football"

That one-and-only look at [Red] Grange in action, which was also my introduction to pro football, taught me a couple of lessons. One was never eat your sandwich as soon as you get to the ball park because then you'll have nothing to eat when you're hungry.

Harold Rosenthal
"Fifty Faces of Football"

Acknowledgments

We owe special gratitude to many people who helped make this book a reality. We thank all of the special tailgaters—friends, family, and even those we hardly knew—who happily shared their fantastic recipes and traditions.

These include Marie Adams, Mary Lou Arteburn, Susan Bowers, John Cadle, Carol Collingsworth, Ruth Collingsworth, Carolyn Columbus, Nancy Craddock, Ellen and David Davies, Bev Davis, Blair Davis, Cliff Davis, Nancy Davis, Paige Davis, Sue Davis, Amy Dean, Mary Fetzer, Evelyn Flynt, LaRue Hanks, Arnelle Haynes, Elizabeth Hill, Kathryn Hoover, Sheri Jordan, Ken Knight, Carol Day Looney, Joyce Looney, Patrick Looney, Rebecca Looney, Paula Lewis, Tom Matte, Denise McDonald, Jesse K. McDonald, Sharon McDonald, Jane Moore, Gloria Petro, Cheryl Reagan, Clay Rossi, Joan Sale, Elaine Sasser, Shanna Rivera Sasser, Vera Sale, Miriam Shanley, Claire Steagall, Leslie Vinson, Sadie Voyles, Anne Walker, Dianne Wade, Scott "Dawg" Walker, and Ruth Westbrooks.

Others shared their talents in a variety of ways, including Charles Belflower, Rachael Bianco, Tim Blalock, Butch Bowers, Rusty and Celia Brien, Molly and Russ Brien, John Brown, Mike Childs, John Dalton, Harriet Jordan, Elaine Kalber, Chris and Jean Lane, Chris and Erin Looney, Dave Looney, Paul Looney, Betsy and Robin Sorrell, Leslie Sorrell, and Tom and Janet Strnad.

We offer special thanks to David and Joanne Sloan of Vision Press for believing in this project and making this book possible. Their suggestions, insights, and expertise were invaluable.

Contents

FOOD AND SPORTS
The Ultimate American Pastime   1

1   PREGAME WARM-UPS
    Beverages and Nibblets   3

2   OPENING KICKOFF
    Breads, Spreads, and Dips   29

3   FIRST QUARTER DRIVE
    Sandwiches   49

4   SECOND QUARTER DOMINATION
    Salads   61

5   HALFTIME PEP TALK
    Soups and Stews   77

6   THIRD QUARTER COMEBACK
    Meats and Main Dishes   91

7   FOURTH QUARTER STAND
    Cookies and Desserts   117

8   VICTORY PARTY
    Tips for a Winning Tailgate   143

Index   163

❦

Food and Sports:
The Ultimate American Pastime

It's only natural that tailgating outdoors before and after autumn ball games became a beloved tradition of American football.

After all, the best gatherings of friends and family always include great food. And food is synonymous with sports in America. What would baseball be without hot dogs and peanuts, or basketball games without popcorn?

Can you imagine college football weekends without pregame picnicking?

Kim envisioned a tailgate recipe book in 1988 during a University of Georgia home football game in Athens. We had taken some homemade eggrolls to our tailgate party, and several people asked us for the recipe.

"Wouldn't it be wonderful," Kim asked, "if we assembled tailgate recipes in book form for present and future generations of tailgaters to try and enjoy?"

We soon began collecting family favorites and recipes from tailgaters at college campuses across the South. In the process, we discovered great stories and fascinating Game Day traditions.

The recipes and stories in this book confirm what we had discovered in the 23 years we've tailgated at Georgia games and at other campuses: watching the pageantry and traditions of college football is great fun, even if you're not a fan of the game. And everyone loves the foods.

With this guide, you will never again fret over what to take to a picnic! All the beloved recipes in this book are "Game Day" tested. Each wonderful edible will keep you craving more.

We have divided *Southern Tailgating* into eight major sections.

• In Chapter 1, "Pregame Warm-ups," you'll find refreshing beverages and mouth-watering nibblets.

- In Chapter 2, "Opening Kickoff," you'll find wonderful breads, spreads, and dips from which to choose.
- Chapter 3, "First Quarter Drive," offers a variety of unbeatable sandwiches that are proven winners.
- In Chapter 4, "Second Quarter Domination," features delicious salads for everyone at your pregame picnics.
- Chapter 5, "Halftime Pep Talk," features soups and stews, both hot and cold. These dishes are easily prepared and guaranteed to please.
- In Chapter 6, "Third Quarter Comeback," discover some of the South's finest barbecue and other recipes for meat lovers.
- Chapter 7, "Fourth Quarter Stand," offers cookies and desserts to satisfy any sweet tooth.
- We close with Chapter 8, "Victory Party," which offers tips for a winning tailgate party and some suggested Game Day menus.

Woven within these chapters are stories of on- and off-field glories and blunders, football anecdotes, tailgating memories, and the odd and exciting Game Day traditions that make Southern college football such a glorious fall pastime.

Pregame Warm-ups

1

Beverages
and
Nibblets

NOTES

❧ 1 ❧

Beverages and Nibblets

Beverages are always in demand at a tailgate picnic. Favorite drinks, ranging from flavored iced teas, to fruit punches, to ice cold beer, disappear faster than Emmett Smith in open field. There can never be too many soft drinks or tea, especially on hot Game Days, which are common in the South well into September.

It's a good idea to bring sufficient beverages for yourself and those who arrive with you, plus enough for two others. Then share freely and wash down those mouth-watering nibblets!

ICED DRINKS

OPENING KICKOFF ICED TEA
GEORGIA BULLDOG

3 quarts medium-strength tea
1 (12-ounce) can frozen lemonade
1/2 cup sugar
1 quart ginger ale

Mix first 3 ingredients and chill. Pour in ginger ale at last minute and serve over crushed ice. Serves 15 to 20.

APPLE ICED TEA
TENNESSEE VOLUNTEER

1 tub Crystal Light iced tea flavor diet soft drink mix
4 cups apple juice

4 cups water
Ice cubes

Place Crystal Light in a large plastic container. Add apple juice and water; stir to dissolve Crystal Light. Serve over ice. Makes 8 servings.

CAROL LOONEY'S LEGENDARY TEA

Many special foods or beverages served at family tailgate parties in the South become so beloved, even *legendary*, that the "regular" picnickers absolutely crave them. And pity the tailgater who forgets to bring these favorites to the table at least twice each new season.

Carol Day Looney, of Winterville, Georgia, serves an iced tea each autumn that's simply irresistible to friends who annually chug it. Our crew in Athens shrugs off colas to devour Carol's tea almost as soon as it arrives in two signature plastic milk jugs. Carol's husband Paul says the recipe, which he claims he doesn't know, is as guarded a secret as Coca-Cola and Kentucky Fried Chicken.

"If you knew how much sugar I put in my tea," admits Carol, "you would not drink it."

YELLOW JACKET CITRUS FIZZ PUNCH
GEORGIA TECH YELLOW JACKET

1 (6-ounce) can frozen grapefruit juice concentrate
1 (6-ounce) can frozen orange juice concentrate
1/4 cup lemon juice
3 cups water
24 ounces ginger ale
Ice cubes

Thaw frozen grapefruit and orange juice concentrates. Mix in lemon juice and water. Pour into large pitcher or plastic punch bowl at the picnic. Add ginger ale and ice. Yield: 16 1/2-cup servings.

SUSAN'S SUPER SODA

Susan Bowers, of Columbia, South Carolina, is famous for a Game Day beverage she calls the "South Carolina Gamecock Super Soda." Susan, a Georgia Bulldog by birth but a Gamecock by marriage, mixes a cup of Russian vodka to a gallon of fresh-squeezed lemonade.

"I've given birth to three Gamecocks, and I'm married to another one; so I guess our house is more Gamecock than Bulldog," she says. "But once a Bulldog, *always* a Bulldog!"

"And when the Gamecocks have to play the Bulldogs," quips Susan, "I add another cup of vodka."

WAR EAGLE TEA
AUBURN WAR EAGLE

7 tea bags
1 (6-ounce) can frozen lemonade
1 (6-ounce) can frozen orange juice concentrate
1 cup unsweetened pineapple juice
1 quart water

Boil 7 tea bags in 1 quart water. Steep for 30 minutes. Add 1 cup sugar. Add the juices and lemonade. Mix thoroughly. Serve cold. Makes 1 gallon.

CRANBERRY APPLE COOLER
GEORGIA BULLDOG

1 quart cranberry juice cocktail
2 (3-inch) sticks cinnamon
4 to 5 whole cloves
1 (16-ounce) can frozen apple concentrate
2 cups water
Mint leaves

In a large saucepan, combine 1/2 of the cranberry juice and all of the cinnamon and cloves. Bring to boiling. Reduce heat. Simmer, covered, for 10 minutes. Remove from heat. Remove and discard cinnamon and cloves. Stir in remaining cranberry juice, apple juice, and water. Cover and chill for several hours or overnight. When serving, garnish with mint leaves. Makes 5 (12-ounce) servings.

LIME TIDE
ALABAMA CRIMSON TIDE

1 lemon-lime 2-liter soft drink
2 cups lime sherbet

Mix together in blender. Serve immediately or chill in refrigerator. A thirst quencher on warm September Saturdays.

LONG-HAIRED PLAYERS

The late William J. Latimer, Class of 1906, is responsible for what is known about the origin of the Clemson Tigers nickname. Professor Walter Merritt Riggs, who coached Clemson's first varsity football team in 1896 and who also served as head coach again in 1899, is said to have "planted the seed" for the school's nickname. In referring to the players from that first team, Latimer said, "Due to the lack of helmets and head protection, they (the players) wore long hair. These long manes might have gained them the name of Lions had it not been for the orange and purple striped jerseys and stockings that resembled tigers. The latter nickname seemed to stick."

BUSH WACKER
FLORIDA STATE SEMINOLE

1 shot rum
1/2 shot kahlua
1/2 shot creme de cacao
1/2 cup milk
2 cups ice

Blend all ingredients until milkshake texture forms.

BURGUNDY APPLE PUNCH
ALABAMA CRIMSON TIDE

1/2 gallon California Burgundy
1 quart apple juice
1 quart ginger ale
1 cup sugar
2 tablespoons lemon juice

Dissolve sugar in apple juice and chill. Add chilled Burgundy and lemon juice. Add ginger ale when ready to serve. Serves 35.

HIGH-TECH TAILGATING

In Atlanta, a saloon called Manuel's Tavern, named for an avid Georgia Tech fan of Lebanese decent, became a legendary watering hole for opposing fans before and after Tech games.

A favorite tradition for Tech and Georgia fans was the display of the winning school's mascot's photo after the annual cross-state bloodletting.

When Georgia won, a photo of a Bulldog was placed over a wooden bar. In the years that Tech won, a Yellow Jacket was mounted on the wall. The next year, if the other team won, its fans were permitted to pull down the photo and burn it in the street.

The Varsity, a fast food legend near Grant Field famous for such heart-stopping foods as frosted oranges, chili dogs, and greasy fries, feeds hundreds of hungry fans arriving for games on Tech's urban campus.

MARY LOU'S SPECIAL
GEORGIA BULLDOG

2 ounces Russian vodka
Orange juice
1 (10-ounce) glass jar with lid

For many years, Bulldog tailgater Blair Davis of Savannah mixed a special concoction for a favorite friend, Mary Lou Arteburn of Riverdale, Georgia. If Georgia were playing in Athens, you could count on two things:

1. Blair Davis would arrive at the picnic site first.
2. Blair would mix Mary Lou's Special.

Here are Blair's instructions: Place vodka in jar and add orange juice to fill. Close lid tightly and place in right-hand corner of ice chest so it is easily accessible when Mary Lou arrives. Next come greetings and hugs, then GET OUT THE JAR!

This practice works with any friend or loved one, especially those too embarrassed to mix their own.

ORANGE SANGRIA
TENNESSEE VOLUNTEER

1 orange
1/4 cup sugar
2 cups orange juice
1 (25.4-ounce) bottle Burgundy, chilled
1/2 cup Triple Sec or other orange-flavored liqueur

Slice orange in half. Cut 1 half into 3 slices. Quarter each slice and reserve for garnish. Carefully cut off the thin outer peel of the other half with a vegetable peeler. Combine orange peel and sugar in bowl. Mash peel with a spoon. Stir in remaining ingredients; cover and chill for 15 minutes. Remove peel and serve over ice. Serves 6 to 8.

HOT DRINKS

HOT COCOA FOR A CROWD
NORTH CAROLINA TARHEEL

1 1/2 cups sugar
1 1/4 cups Hershey's cocoa
1/2 teaspoon salt
3/4 cup hot water
4 quarts (1 gallon) milk
1 tablespoon vanilla extract

In 6-quart saucepan, combine sugar, cocoa, and salt; gradually add hot water. Cook over medium heat, stirring constantly, until mixture boils. Boil and stir 2 minutes. Add milk; reduce heat to serving temperature, stirring occasionally. DO NOT BOIL. Remove from heat; add vanilla. Serve hot. Makes about 22 (6-ounce) servings.

CRIMSON CIDER
ALABAMA CRIMSON TIDE

1 gallon of apple cider
1 quart of water
8 ounces of cinnamon candies
1 cup sugar (vary to desired sweetness)
1 teaspoon cinnamon

Heat water to boiling. Then on moderate heat, add cinnamon candies. Stir until candies melt, making sure they don't stick to bottom of pan. Add cider and sugar. Stir until sugar is dissolved. Add 1 teaspoon cinnamon. Continue to heat until mixtures comes to boil. Remove immediately and serve. Makes approximately 20 servings.

THE CALLING

Highway 16 north from Savannah is a long, seemingly endless road stretching from Georgia's sun-draped coastline through rural southeast Georgia toward Macon.

From Macon, the road snakes north up U.S. 441 through the village birthplace of writer Joel Chandler Harris into the sloping hills of Athens—a route nearly parallel to the historic antebellum trail.

It's a long drive from Savannah to Athens, a four-hour journey past fields and farms and roadside vegetable stands.

In early fall, the sun sometimes weighs so heavily on the south Georgia countryside that the road seems to waver like a frothy tide retreating into the sea.

It's not a drive you'd choose to make every weekend—that Savannah to Athens pilgrimage—unless some inner calling, so strong you can't ignore it beckons you forward.

Sue Brown Davis of Savannah has made that pilgrimage every September through December for nearly 35 years. For her, the calling surfaces in late summer, and sometimes as early as July.

"I want to go back, I want to go back, U-G, U-G, G-E-O-R-G-I-A!" That's how a lyricist communicated the feeling, an urging really, to return to one's roots.

Behind it all is an annual ritual that holds families together and keeps good friends in touch.

Sue and her late husband, Blair Wilson Davis, cherished the annual tradition of tailgating before and after University of Georgia football games. Together they would gather with friends and children behind a parked car at a picnic table covered with food and drink for all to share.

Blair was the driving force behind the pregame picnics. He loved to joke and laugh with old friends, enjoy a drink, and soak in the sounds and excitement of thousands of red-clad enthusiasts gathered about the extensive Athens campus sharing similar experiences.

As the years passed, many of the Davises' peers and tailgate buddies passed away. Younger generations took their place at the picnics. Blair's enjoyment of the fall ritual continued.

Sue's longtime tailgate spot remains a shade tree atop a grassy hill behind the brick Fine Arts building. The hill overlooks the University Bookstore and the Tate Student Center. Sanford Stadium is a short stroll southeast from the hill.

"Blair always said that even though he loved attending the games, the really important part of it was the family and friends getting together," Sue said.

Blair's determination to continue the tradition of tailgating before and after his beloved Bulldogs played led he and Sue up Highway 16 from Savannah to Athens each fall for three decades. The Davises epitomized the ultimate football faithful's unwriten creed: Get to the game early at all costs.

You could almost bet your game ticket that Blair and Sue would arrive to the games first, reserving two or three parking spaces for other family members. And, barring extreme weather, you could expect to see Blair proudly wearing his red blazer with a Georgia emblem sewn on the front pocket.

The Bulldog pregame football festivities began in earnest after World War II, when Blair and Sue settled in Athens.

"On football weekends our little house would be bursting at the seams with football guests," recalled Sue. "Lunch was an `everybody welcome' affair on Game Day."

In those early years, Sue and Blair usually drove to Sue's grandmother's house on Doughery Street, parked, and walked to the stadium.

The couple moved to south Georgia in 1950 and, despite the difficulties of traveling with three small children (including an infant), returned to Athens for most games. They would drop their children at an aunt's house in Atlanta and drive to Athens.

The journey proved too wearing for a young family, however, and for several years the games took lower priority.

During the mid-1960s, the university added the club section to Sanford Stadium. The family continued to gather with friends behind the Fine Arts building near the Grady journalism school.

Blair Davis passed away the week of the 1988 Georgia-Florida game in Jacksonville. He had postponed major surgery for a week to attend what would become his final Bulldog game: the Georgia-Kentucky game in Lexington.

Each season Blair planned one away game trip with three male friends, another tradition so important he felt his surgery could wait. The surgery never took place.

Blair's family buried him in his red Bulldog blazer in Savannah while Georgia battled Florida two hours south. Bulldog play-by-play announcer Larry Munson announced the news of Blair's death and funeral during the radio broadcast of the game.

Children and grandchildren still share great food and memories with Sue and other original tailgaters at the annual pregame gatherings. Following Blair's example, passersby are still invited to "come on over" and celebrate one of life's true pleasures.

OZARK AUTUMN SPICED TEA
ARKANSAS RAZORBACK

2 cups orange-flavored instant breakfast drink
1 cup sugar
1/2 cup instant tea with lemon
1 teaspoon ground cinnamon
1 teaspoon ground cloves
Dash of nutmeg
Dash of allspice

Mix all ingredients together; store in a tightly sealed jar or tin. Makes 3 to 4 cups of instant tea mix. Use 2 teaspoons (or vary according to strength desired) per cup of hot water. Delicious on November football mornings.

RUSHING YARDS SPICE TEA
MISSISSIPPI STATE BULLDOG

2 cups Tang
1 cup instant sweetened tea
3 ounces instant dry lemonade mix
1/2 teaspoon cinnamon
1/2 teaspoon ground cloves
1/2 teaspoon nutmeg

Mix all ingredients. Store in an airtight tin or glass jar. Add 1-2 tablespoons to 1 cup boiling water for hot tea. Can be mixed in larger amounts and kept hot in a thermos.

WHO IS LOONEY?

A famous question, never answered, originated after a fight in 1896 between players from Vanderbilt and the University of Nashville: "Who hit Looney?"

NIBBLETS

POPCORN POTPOURRI
GEORGIA BULLDOG

FIESTA BUTTERED POPCORN:

Combine 1 teaspoon melted corn oil margarine, 1/8 teaspoon chili powder, a dash of garlic salt, and a dash of paprika. Toss 1 1/2 cups warm popped popcorn with melted butter mixture until coated.

LEMON-BASIL BUTTERED POPCORN:

Combine 1 teaspoon melted corn oil margarine, 1/8 teaspoon dried basil (crushed) and a few drops of lemon juice. Toss 1 1/2 cups warm popped popcorn with melted mixture until coated. Sprinkle lightly with salt, if desired.

PARMESAN POPCORN:

Combine 1 teaspoon melted corn oil margarine and 1/8 teaspoon parmesan cheese. Toss 1 1/4 cups warm popped popcorn with the melted butter mixture until melted.

CURRY COATED POPCORN:

Combine 1 teaspoon melted corn oil margarine and 1/8 teaspoon curry powder. Toss 1 1/4 cups warm popped popcorn with the melted butter mixture until well coated.

GREEN AND GOLD BUTTERED POPCORN:

Toss 1 1/4 cups warm popped popcorn with 1 teaspoon melted corn oil margarine until coated. Sprinkle with 1 teaspoon snipped parsley and 1/2 teaspoon finely chopped chives. Toss to mix. Sprinkle lightly with salt, if desired.

Make desired flavor of popcorn. Store in baggies and tie with ribbons of school colors. Grab a bag on the way to the game!

When Alabama Coach Bear Bryant retired after the 1982 season, he was the all-time leader in collegiate coaching victories with 323. Although his total has since been surpassed, Bryant still holds the record for the most victories among Division I-A coaches. The Paul Bryant Museum, which holds memorabilia from Bryant's 25 years at Alabama, is one of the state's main tourist attractions.

ROASTED PECANS
CLEMSON TIGER

1 pound pecans (4 cups)
1/2 stick butter or margarine
1 tablespoon Durkees seasoning salt

Melt butter and stir in seasoning salt. Place pecans in a microwavable dish and pour melted butter mixture over pecans. Cook in microwave for 3 minutes. Stir. Cook 3 more minutes. Stir again. Cook a few minutes if butter has not been absorbed. *NO HUNGRY FAN CAN EAT JUST ONE!*

GOAL POST GOODIES
MISSISSIPPI STATE BULLDOG

Ham (cubed)
Pineapple chunks
Whole sweet pickles

Keep the above ingredients separate until just before tailgate time. Place one piece of each ingredient on a toothpick for a quick and tasty finger food.

AIR BALL

The University of New Mexico was the first college football team to fly to a game.

Occidental College, of California, invited New Mexico Coach Roy Johnson to take his team west to play Oxy in a huge new stadium in Pasadena.

The game at the Rose Bowl would be played on a Friday night under lights, which were a novelty in 1929.

Johnson decided the trip to California might help recruiting and would be educational to his players. During that same summer, aviator Charles Lindbergh helped organize Transcontinental Air Transport, which included a flight from Albuquerque to Los Angeles.

The plane only sat 18 people, and Johnson, fearing air sickness, put his subs on the flight to LA. His best 11 players journeyed to California by train. The plan was to switch places on the return trip so that everyone on the team would get a plane ride.

The subs, traveling by plane, arrived at the Rose Bowl early enough to adjust to the lights. The trainbound starters didn't, and the glaring light created vision problems for New Mexico players throughout the game.

Oxy whipped New Mexico 26-0 that night in front of 17,000 spectators. Johnson's team, however, became the first aerial team in history.

PARTY WINGS CHILI
ALABAMA CRIMSON TIDE

4 pounds chicken wings
1 package McCormick chili mix
1/4 cup corn meal
3/4 teaspoon salt
2 teaspoons parsley flakes

Combine all dry ingredients in bowl and mix well. Coat chicken wings in this mixture and place in a single layer in well-greased baking dish. Bake at 350 degrees for 25 minutes. Turn wings over and bake until tender, about 10 minutes.

AIRING IT OUT

Former Auburn Coach Pat Dye said there once was a tradition in the Southeastern Conference of head coaches settling differences among themselves behind closed doors.

Dye said he learned of the tradition during his first SEC meeting in Destin, Florida. It was one of the last annual coaches' meetings attended by the late Alabama coach Paul Bryant.

Dye, a former University of Georgia lineman, said Georgia's Vince Dooley told him that the coaches used to end the SEC meetings by asking everyone except the head coaches to leave the room.

"And they'd get across from one another and say, `You SOB, you know you did this or that...,'" Dye recalled Dooley telling him. The coaches aired their differences, talked about whatever was bothering them, and tried to settle it in the room, said Dye.

SOUTHERN COMFORT DAWGS
GEORGIA BULLDOG

2 packages hot dogs
1 (14-ounce) bottle ketchup
1 cup brown sugar
1/4 cup bourbon or Southern Comfort

Cut each hot dog into 4 pieces. Mix ketchup, brown sugar, and bourbon in a crock pot or slow cooker. Add hot dogs. Cook on high heat approximately 45 minutes. Cook on low heat for 1-1/2 hours. Serve with toothpicks.

DAWG BITES
MISSISSIPPI STATE BULLDOG

1 pound chicken breast filets (deboned and skinned)
Meat tenderizer
Paprika
Chili powder (to taste)
Flour
Oil

Cut the chicken into bite-sized pieces. Sprinkle with meat tenderizer, paprika, and chili powder. Roll in flour and place in a pan with hot oil. Cook until just brown on each side. Serve with sweet and sour sauce on a Bulldog tray.

TAILGATERS' MINIATURE REUBENS
VANDERBILT COMMODORE

24 slices cocktail rye bread
3 tablespoons Thousand Island dressing
24 small, thin slices cooked corn beef
1 (8-ounce) can sauerkraut or 1 cup refrigerated sauerkraut,
    drained
3/4 cup shredded Swiss cheese (3 ounces)

Preheat broiler, if necessary. Place oven rack 3 to 5 inches from heating element. Arrange single layer of bread on an ungreased baking sheet. Spread each with thin coating of dressing. Place 1 slice corned beef on each. Top evenly with sauerkraut. Sprinkle Swiss cheese evenly over sauerkraut. Broil until bubbly, 2 or 3 minutes. Serve hot. Makes 24 servings.

GOAL LINE CHEESE STRAWS
AUBURN TIGER

2 cups Rice Krispies
2 cups grated cheddar cheese
2 cups flour
1 1/2 sticks margarine
2 teaspoons salt
2 teaspoons red pepper (optional)

Mix ingredients. Shape into balls and flatten. Bake at 350 degrees for 8 to 10 minutes. Makes 4 dozen.

ALABAMA'S FIRST

Alabama played its first football game on a Friday afternoon in Birmingham in 1892. The opponent that day at the old Lakeview Park was a team picked from Professor Tyler's School and some Birmingham area high schools. The Varsity, as Alabama was called that day, won, 56-0.

CRUNCHY CHEESE WAFERS
GEORGIA BULLDOG

2 cups grated sharp cheese
3/4 teaspoon salt
1 cup margarine, softened
2 cups all purpose flour
1/8 teaspoon sugar
1/4 teaspoon cayenne pepper
2 cups Rice Krispies
1 teaspoon Worcestershire sauce
1/2 teaspoon hot sauce

Blend cheese and butter in a large bowl. Sift flour, sugar, cayenne pepper and salt into cheese and butter mixture. Add remaining ingredients. Work dough with pastry blender or hands until well blended. Pinch dough into 1-inch balls. Place on ungreased cookie sheet. Press down with a fork. Bake in 350 degree oven for 10 to 12 minutes. Cool and store in sealed container. Handle gently to avoid breaking.

CLEMSON'S BEST

John Heisman, the coach for which the trophy is named, led Clemson to its first undefeated season in 1900. He coached at Clemson for four years. The school celebrated its first national football championship in 1981, with a 22-15 win over Nebraska in the Orange Bowl.

NUT PARTY MIX
GEORGIA BULLDOG

1 1/2 sticks margarine
1 package pumpkin seeds
1 teaspoon garlic salt
1 teaspoon celery salt
1 tablespoon Worcestershire sauce
1/2 box Rice Chex
1/2 box Cheerios
3/4 box pretzelettes
1 cup pecans or peanuts, or both (twice the nut content is best)

Melt margarine. Add seeds and seasonings. Mix in cereals, pretzelettes, and nuts. Bake about 1 hour at 225 degrees, stirring frequently. Remove when cooled and store in tightly fitted container.

BOWKNOTS
GEORGIA SOUTHERN EAGLE

1 loaf fresh sandwich bread (white or whole wheat), thinly sliced
1 (10-1/2 ounce) can condensed cream of mushroom soup, undiluted
12 bacon strips (uncooked), cut in half
24 toothpicks

Trim all crust off bread. Spread soup on 1 side of bread slices, being careful to cover edges. Roll each slice from one corner to opposite corner. Wrap bacon strip around middle of each roll and secure with toothpick. Place on cookie sheet and bake at 250 degrees for 1 hour. The Bowknots will be dry, crisp and delicious. Makes 2 dozen appetizers.

Prepared Bowknots may be frozen before baking. Place on a flat pan; when frozen solid, transfer to freezer bags. Bake without thawing, extending baking time about 15 minutes. Other condensed soups, such as cream of asparagus or chicken, can be substituted for mushroom.

ALMOST TOO LATE

The death of Georgia tailback Richard Von Gammon from head injuries sustained during a game against Virginia in 1895 prompted the Georgia legislature to overwhelmingly pass an anti-football bill.

Only a letter from Von Gammon's mother to Georgia Governor W.Y. Atkinson asking the governor to veto the bill saved the game.

Von Gammon's mother wrote that she believed her "boy's death should not be used to defeat the most cherished object of his life...." That year, 18 boys died on U.S. football fields.

The deaths caused President Theodore Roosevelt to tell football officials to "open up or close up," paving the way for rules changes and the legalization of the forward pass.

SIMPLY GREAT DEVILED EGGS
FLORIDA STATE SEMINOLE

6 eggs, hard boiled
1/4 cup mayonnaise
1 tablespoon sweet pickle relish
1/2 teaspoon Worcestershire sauce
1/4 teaspoon salt
1/4 teaspoon dry mustard
Paprika

Slice eggs in half lengthwise and carefully remove yolks. Mash yolks and mayonnaise. Add remaining ingredients, except parsley; stir well. Stuff egg whites with egg mixture. Garnish eggs with paprika.

BACK PAY

Former Georgia coach Vince Dooley used to fine his assistant coaches if they arrived late to staff meetings. Beginning with 50 cents for the first minute, Dooley increased the fines for every minute the coach missed. At year's end, he threw "Tardy Parties" with the fines he collected.

HIDDEN VALLEY RANCH QUESADILLAS
GEORGIA BULLDOG

1 package Hidden Valley Ranch milk recipe Original Ranch
   salad dressing mix
3/4 cup mayonnaise
1/3 cup milk
1/3 cup chunky salsa
3 cups shredded Monterey Jack cheese
10 (10)-inch flour tortillas
Vegetable oil

Blend together the first 5 ingredients. Refrigerate 1 hour. Spread mixture over 5 tortillas, covering with remaining tortillas. Brush tops with oil. Broil on a baking sheet until golden (1 minute). Turn and repeat process. Broil until cheese is melted. Cut each into 8 wedges.

CRUSTED PEANUTS
ALABAMA CRIMSON TIDE

1/2 cup water
1 cup sugar
3 1/2 cups peanuts with husks on

Bring water and sugar to boil. Add peanuts. Continue boiling, stirring constantly until all moisture is gone. Place peanuts on greased pan, salt lightly, and bake at 250 degrees for about 30 minutes, stirring every 10 minutes.

BLAIR'S TOASTED PECANS
GEORGIA BULLDOG

White of egg
Rounded teaspoon salt
1 teaspoon milk
1 teaspoon water
1/2 teaspoon sugar

Dip nuts in mix and bake for 15 minutes at 250 degrees. Turn oven off and let pecans remain in oven for 30 minutes more.

BULLDOG NUT PASTRIES
GEORGIA BULLDOG

1 cup dark brown sugar
2 eggs
3 tablespoons butter or margarine, melted
1 teaspoon vanilla
1 1/2 cups nuts

Mix above ingredients. Put into uncooked pastry shell and cook in 350 degree oven approximately 20 minutes, or until crust is golden brown. Ready-to-bake tart shells may be used, or ready-to-bake pie shell pastry from dairy counter. Pastry for a 2-crust pie will make 12 tart shells.

"DOG-GONE" PUPPY CHOW
AUBURN TIGER

1 stick margarine
1 6-ounce bag chocolate chips
Small jar smooth peanut butter
Regular-sized box Crispex cereal
1 box powdered sugar

Melt margarine and chips together. Stir in peanut butter. Gently stir in box of Crispex. Pour powdered sugar into large paper bag and add cereal mixture. Take outside and shake until coated. *Makes a "ton" and is habit forming.*

MISSISSIPPI PUPPY CHOW
MISSISSIPPI STATE BULLDOG

8 ounces dark raisins
8 ounces white raisins
1 pound dry roasted mixed nuts
8 ounces dry roasted peanuts
1 pound plain M&M candies

Mix all the above ingredients in a large, colorful bowl with a secure lid. Place in an easy-to-reach place during the tailgate party so handfuls can be grabbed.

NO MORE 'BAMA 'RAMMER'

One of Alabama's most popular cheers, "Rammer Jammer," has twice been banned by athletic directors who fear the cheer taunts opposing teams and fans and could lead to fighting.

"Hey-y-y Auburn (or Tennessee, or whoever)! *We're going to beat the hell out of you! Rammer jammer yellowhammer, Give'em hell Alabama!"*

Steve Sloan, Alabama athletic director in the late 1980s, was the first to ban the cheer. Sloan, one of Bear Bryant's former players, believed the cheer lacked class.

In 1994, athletic director Hootie Ingram, who had allowed the cheer to be played at the end of a game that was well in hand, banned it again.

During Bryant's last three years at Alabama, the cheer

was played often and loud—before, during, and after football games. Sloan said Bryant was not "really into cheers."

Ironically, the music and other words were copied from Mississippi during a 1980 game when Sloan was coaching the Rebels.

GRANOLA
GEORGIA BULLDOG

1/2 cup salad oil
1/2 cup powdered milk
1/2 cup honey
1/2 cup whole wheat flour
2 tablespoons molasses
1/2 cup bran
2 1/2 cups rolled oats
1/2 cup shredded coconut
1/2 cup chopped pecans
1/2 cup sesame seeds
1/2 cup sunflower seeds
1/2 cup raisins

* May substitute dried, mixed fruit for final ingredients.

Mix oil, honey, and molasses. Heat until mixture thins. Add dry ingredients, except raisins. Spread on cookie sheets and bake at 325 degrees for 15 to 20 minutes until slightly brown. Stir 2 or 3 times during baking. Do not over bake. Remove from oven and allow to cool, stirring occasionally. Add raisins while slightly warm. Store in tightly closed container.

PIG SOOEY CORN CHEX TREATS
ARKANSAS RAZORBACK

1 cup sugar
1 cup Karo syrup
1 tablespoon margarine
1 teaspoon vanilla
1 cup peanut butter
5-6 cups Corn Chex cereal

Heat first three ingredients to boiling. Remove from heat. Add
vanilla and peanut butter. Then add Corn Chex. Place in 13 x 9 x
3 pan and pat down with buttered spatula. Let cool and serve.

FOOTBALL IN THE SOUTH—1898
—From *Outing* sports magazine, 1898

The Southern Intercollegiate Athletic Association, with a
territory spreading from South Carolina to Texas and from Kentucky to Louisiana, embracing such representative universities
as University of Georgia, University of the South and Vanderbilt University, has formulated rules governing the methods of
play and conduct of the players. The representatives of the colleges have entered upon the subject of modification of play in a
spirit of earnestness, and they hope to avoid accidents to players and reduce the casualties to a minimum.

The University of Georgia team is again in the field, despite the attempt by the Georgia Legislature to abolish the
game in the Cracker State. The team she will put in the field
this year is especially strong, having replaced the vacancies in
the line by good material, Captain Walden himself playing
one of the tackles. Captain Walden made a great reputation
last year in his strong defensive play against Virginia's heavy
team. Tichenor will be at quarter again and will direct the
play from the signal center. Jones will do their punting again
this year, and is probably the quickest full-back in the South.
Moore, the big half, is back again, and plays a strong game on
offense but is careless on defense.

Vanderbilt will make a good showing this year; Goodson,
last year's star quarter, will captain from his old position. The
positions to be filled by the loss of Connell, Farrall, Boogher
and Crutchfield is a problem for Captain Goodson, but with the
new material, some of which gives great promise, there is little
doubt but that Vanderbilt will play a creditable season.

At North Carolina the men are being coached by Reynolds,
of Princeton, and, while Captain Belden has not returned, many
of the old team are in harness again. Belden's strong kicking
will be missed, but Rogers may go from quarter to full. Gregory,
the great end and captain of Carolina '95, is again in college
and, if he does not play, will be of valuable assistance to Coach

Reynolds.

Virginia has entered upon a new era in football, abolishing the hired coach system, and plunged into the arena on her own basis, using her alumni exclusively for coaches. The progress of the Virginia team will be watched with considerable interest, since it is the first Southern college to adopt the home-coach system.

The North Carolina Schedule

Oct. 1   Guilford College
Oct. 8   Mechanical College
Oct. 12   Greensboro Athletic Club
Oct. 15   Mebane School
Oct. 22   University of Georgia
Nov. 4   Alabama Polytechnic
Nov. 24   University of Virginia

🍴

Opening Kickoff

2

Breads,
Spreads
and Dips

NOTES

❧ 2 ❧

Breads, Spreads, and Dips

Enjoy some great dips, spreads, and breads while swapping some football stories at your next tailgate party.

SPREADS AND DIPS

TOMATO AND BACON SPREAD
GEORGIA BULLDOG

1 (8-ounce) package cream cheese, softened
1 medium tomato, peeled, seeded, and finely chopped
2 teaspoons prepared mustard
1/2 teaspoon celery salt
1/4 cup green pepper, finely chopped
6 slices bacon, cooked crisp, drained, and crumbled
Assorted vegetable dippers

In a small bowl, stir together cream cheese, mustard, and celery salt. Stir in remaining ingredients. Cover and chill. Serve with vegetable dippers.

CREAM CHEESE AND PINEAPPLE SPREAD OR DIP
SOUTH CAROLINA GAMECOCK

1 stick margarine
1 (8-ounce) block cream cheese
1 (15-ounce) can pineapple, drained
2 tablespoons cornstarch
2 tablespoons Miracle Whip

Melt butter and cream cheese over low heat, stirring constantly. When melted, add pineapple and mix well. Add cornstarch and blend until smooth. Cool; then add Miracle Whip. Mix well and refrigerate.

This youth goes to the game fortified by at least a dozen Royal Baking Powder hot cakes, and he looks like a winner.

Athletes, and those subject to severe physical strain, were formerly deprived of a good share of the pleasures of the table, because so many of the things they would have liked to eat were prejudicial to healthy stomachs and strong muscles.

Royal Baking Powder has changed all that. With it the most desirable of our everyday foods—all kinds of hot breads, hot griddle-cakes, pot-pies, puddings, muffins and doughnuts—are made perfectly digestible and wholesome. Even the hot buckwheat cake—when rightly made the most delicious of all the winter griddle-cakes, but which made in the old-fashioned way is the most indigestible—risen with Royal Baking Powder, is a digestible, wholesome, nutritious food.

Royal Baking Powder is made from pure grape cream of tartar, the most healthful of all fruit acids.

Foods raised with Royal Baking Powder are unfermented and may be eaten in their most delicious state, fresh and hot, by persons of all temperaments and occupations, without fear of unpleasant results.

Alum is used as a cheap substitute for cream of tartar in making many baking powders. It is a corrosive acid, condemned by physicians as dangerous to health when taken with the food. Flabby muscles and weak heart are caused by the continuous use of alum food.

Royal Baking Powder advertisement, 1896

HAM SPREAD
GEORGIA BULLDOG

3 cups cooked ham, ground up
3 tablespoons mayonnaise
3 tablespoons mustard
Sweet pickle relish, to taste
Dash Worcestershire sauce
Dash dry mustard

Mix all above well. *Delicious on sandwiches or crackers!*

GATOR BOWL CREAMY FRESH FRUIT DIP
GEORGIA BULLDOG

1 (8-ounce) package cream cheese, softened
1 (7-ounce) jar marshmallow creme
1 tablespoon orange juice
1 teaspoon grated orange peel

Combine ingredients, mixing at medium speed on electric mixer, until well blended. Serve over fruit. Makes 1 1/2 cups.

Variations:
1) Omit orange juice and peel. Add 1 tablespoon almond flavored liqueur.
2) Omit orange juice and peel. Add 1/4 cup chocolate pieces, melted.

THE GROWTH OF A TRADITION

Princeton and Rutgers kicked off the first college game at 3 p.m. on November 6, 1869. Although the game played that day was basically soccer, it's still viewed as the first intercollegiate football contest in America. Rutgers won, 6-4.

Early teams played on dirt fields or grassy commons. Students crowded near the teams around the sidelines or cheered from fences waving hand-stitched pennants.

The crowds grew steadily each season. Schools began erecting wooden bleachers and grandstands to accommodate spectators. The wooden seats were later replaced by concrete stadiums and massive bowls.

As the sport grew increasingly popular, new traditions and pageantry flourished. Alumni began returning to campus en masse for big games against rival teams. Such fans, especially out-of-towners, started arriving early on Game Day. They'd gather on grassy knolls, shaded groves, and parking areas around the stadium to picnic.

As stadiums grew larger to accommodate the demand for tickets, the picnics stretched farther across campus. Fans partied wherever they parked, and tailgating became an institution.

The spirit and color of these Saturday afternoon traditions is now legendary. Students, alumni, and local townsfolk love their team to a fault and identify strongly with its mascots, cheerleaders, fight songs, and marching bands.

CALL THE HOGS SPINACH DIP
ARKANSAS RAZORBACK

1 (10-ounce) package frozen chopped spinach, drained
1 (1 5/8-ounce) Knorrs dried vegetable soup mix
1 (8-ounce) can water chestnuts, chopped
1/2 teaspoon grated onion
1 cup mayonnaise
1 cup sour cream

In a large mixing bowl combine the thawed and thoroughly drained spinach (squeeze all water out of spinach) with the soup mix, water chestnuts, onion, mayonnaise and sour cream. Refrigerate several hours or overnight. Serve with large fritos, sturdy crackers, or raw vegetables. *This recipe will bring out all the hogs.*

REBEL SALSA
MISSISSIPPI REBEL

1 (1-pound) can tomatoes, drained
1 (8-ounce) can tomato sauce
1/2 onion, chopped

1/4 teaspoon garlic (2 cloves)
4 to 7 jalapeno peppers
2 tablespoons vinegar
1 tablespoon sugar
1 teaspoon salt
1 teaspoon pepper

Blend all ingredients in blender. Then add 1 small can chopped green chilies. Refrigerate. Serve with tortilla chips.

ALL-STAR WEST-OF-THE-BORDER DIP
LOUISIANA STATE TIGER

1 (16-ounce) can refried beans (add tabasco or 1/2 package taco seasoning)
1 (6-ounce) carton avocado dip
1 (8-ounce) carton sour cream
1 (4-1/2-ounce) can chopped black olives
2 large tomatoes, diced
8 good-sized scallions, finely chopped
1 (4-ounce) can chopped green chilies
1 1/2 cup (6 ounces) shredded Monterey Jack cheese

Combine beans and taco seasoning mix. Spread bean mixture evenly in 12 x 8 x 2 dish. Layer remaining ingredients in the order listed. Serve with large corn chips.

COCKS CORNER

In Columbia, South Carolina, many Gamecock fans pay a heavy price to park and tailgate party near Williams-Brice Stadium.

At Cocks Corner, a fenced parking lot with a pavilion about 100 yards from the stadium on George Rogers Boulevard, fans purchased a parking spot for $7,500. A typical spot carries a $600 annual mortgage payment. The owner of that tiny piece of real estate also pays property tax.

But they do have fun. Motor homes park, and awnings are set up. Loudspeakers play hip hop or country dance music, and tailgaters draw approving crowds by country line dancing to high tempo tunes.

Behind the south end zone stands, 20 refurbished cabooses, all painted brick red, are parked on rail siding that was bought and renovated by entrepreneurs years ago.

The party cabooses, whose interiors are customized by the owners, were originally sold to diehard football fans and corporations for $45,000 each. Resale prices now near $100,000.

CHEESY BEEF DIP
GEORGIA BULLDOG

1/3 cup chopped pecans
1 1/2 tablespoon melted butter
1 (2 1/2 ounce) jar dried beef
1 (8-ounce) package of cream cheese, softened
2 tablespoons milk
1/4 cup finely chopped green pepper
1/4 cup finely chopped onion
1/4 teaspoon garlic powder
1/2 teaspoon white pepper
1/2 cup sour cream

Saute pecans in butter 3 to 5 minutes. Set aside. Place dried beef in bowl. Chop. Combine cheese and milk in a medium bowl. Beat on medium speed until smooth. Stir in beef, green pepper, onion, garlic, and white pepper. Stir in sour cream. Spoon in casserole. Sprinkle pecans on top. Bake at 350 degrees for 25 minutes. Serve with Triskets or wheat crackers.

CHEESE DIP
CLEMSON TIGER

1 pound velveeta cheese
1 (16-ounce) can tomatoes, drained and chopped
1 (4-ounce) can whole green chilies, drained and chopped
3/4 cup chopped onion
1 teaspoon chili powder

Mix all ingredients. Heat until cheese melts. Serve with tortilla chips. Wonderful *and fattening!*

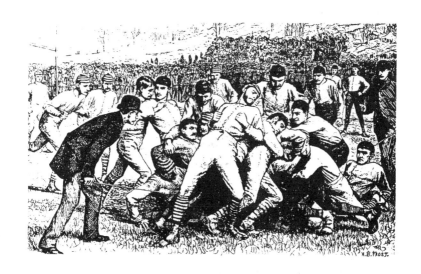

OLÉ DIP
MISSISSIPPI STATE BULLDOG

2 cans refried beans
1 pint sour cream
Lemon juice
Pepper
Garlic powder
Tomatoes, diced
Green onions
Ripe olives
Grated cheese (MSU's cheese, for sure)
1 bottle taco sauce
Lettuce, shredded

Layer the beans, sour cream (seasoned with a little lemon juice, pepper, and garlic powder), tomatoes, onions, olives, cheese, taco sauce, and lettuce in a 13 x 9 inch pan. Serve with tortilla chips.

BEAR'S POEM

The late Alabama Coach Paul "Bear" Bryant usually carried a poem with him. Below was a favorite:

This is the beginning of a new day. God has given me this day to use as I will. I can waste it or use it for good. What I do today is very important because I am exchanging a day of my life for it. When tomorrow comes, this day will be gone forever, leaving something in its place I have traded for it. I want it to be a gain, not loss—good, not evil. Success, not failure, in order that I shall not forget the price I paid for it.

GUACAMOLE DIP
TENNESSEE VOLUNTEER

4 ripe avocados
1 (9-ounce) can Frito Lay's brand picante sauce
2 tablespoons lime juice
2 tablespoons chopped cilantro or parsley
1 medium jalapeno pepper, seeded and chopped (optional)
1/2 teaspoon seasoning salt
2 cloves garlic, minced

Halve avocados; scoop pulp into large bowl and mash with fork. Add remaining ingredients to avocado; stir to blend. Makes about 4 cups.

PIZZA DIP
GEORGIA BULLDOG

1 (8 ounce) package of cream cheese
1 (14-ounce) jar pizza sauce
1/3 cup chopped onion
1 1/2 cups grated mozzarella cheese
1 (16-ounce) can chopped ripe olives
2 ounces chopped pepperoni
Large package corn chips

Preheat oven to 350 degrees. Press cream cheese in bottom of 9-inch glass pie plate. Spread pizza sauce over cream cheese and layer remaining ingredients in order listed. Bake at 350 degrees for 25 minutes. Serve with large corn chips.

STRAWBERRY DIP
FLORIDA STATE SEMINOLE

7-, 9-, or 10-ounce marshmallow creme
3 tablespoons creme de almond
3 tablespoons creme de cacao
1 teaspoon lemon juice

Mix lemon juice and liqueurs in saucepan over low heat. Add marshmallow creme and stir. Heat until well blended. Transfer to fondue pot and serve with fresh strawberries and bananas.

BREADS

BEER BREAD
GEORGIA BULLDOG

1 can beer
3 cups self-rising flour
1 cup sugar
1 stick butter, melted

Mix first 3 ingredients and pour into loaf pan. Pour melted butter on top of batter. Bake at 350 degrees for 1 hour.

BROCCOLI BREAD
GEORGIA BULLDOG

1 box Jiffy corn muffin mix
1 (10-ounce) package broccoli, cooked and drained
1 cup cottage cheese
1 grated onion
1 stick butter or margarine
3 eggs

Mix all ingredients together. Cook at 350 degrees in a greased loaf pan.

MEXICAN CORN BREAD
ARKANSAS RAZORBACK

1 cup yellow corn meal
1 cup sweet milk
3 eggs
3 jalepeno peppers, chopped (vary amount to desired taste)
1/2 cup chopped onions
1 teaspoon garlic powder
1 1/2 cups shredded cheese
1/2 teaspoon salt
1/2 teaspoon soda
1/2 teaspoon sugar
1 cup corn (whole or creamed)
1 small chopped pimentoes)
1/3 cup bacon drippings or corn oil

Mix all ingredients together and cook in greased skillet, 350 degrees for 45 minutes. *YUMMY!*

CHEESE BISCUITS
GEORGIA TECH YELLOW JACKET

2 cups grated cheese (extra sharp)
2 teaspoons baking powder
1 egg
2 cups flour
1/2 teaspoon salt
1/2 teaspoon Crisco

Mix all ingredients and knead until dough is smooth. Roll out and cut. Bake at 425 degrees for 12 to 15 minutes.

THE ORIGINS OF SOUTHERN TAILGATING

The first tailgate parties originated in the South, but not outside a large stadium hours before a big football game.

To find the first American tailgaters, you need only to return to Manassas, Virginia, and the First Battle of Bull Run in July 1861.

In the days preceding the first major clash of Union and Confederate forces, hoards of civilians from Washington followed the federal army into Virginia. The curious Washingtonians, noted historian William C. Davis, wished "to witness the grandest spectacle of their time—the thrashing of the Rebels."

Hundreds of civilians, including congressmen, senators, and ladies with picnic baskets, arrived near the battle scene on horseback and in buggies. These picnickers included Secretary of War Simon Cameron and Mathew Brady, a prominent Washington photographer.

Every few hours, Union soldiers heard train whistles from the nearby junction at Manassas, where Confederate troops under Gen. Joseph E. Johnston briefly detrained enroot from the Shenandoah Valley to the battlefield. Confederate women waited at the Manassas junction to treat the Southern soldiers to refreshments prior to the battle.

RAISIN BRAN MUFFINS
MISSISSIPPI STATE BULLDOG

1 (15-ounce) box Raisin Bran
3 cups sugar
5 cups flour
4 eggs, beaten
3/4 cup oil
1 quart buttermilk
Dash of cinnamon
Pecans, chopped (optional)

Mix cereal, sugar, and flour in large mixing bowl. Add eggs, oil, nuts, cinnamon, and buttermilk. Mix well. Put into muffin pans and bake at 400 degrees for about 20 minutes. (Batter will keep for up to 6 weeks in the refrigerator.) Cover warm muffins with foil and take to those morning tailgate parties.

OSCEOLA AND RENEGADE

A Florida State tradition is focused around Chief Osceola and Renegade as they lead the FSU football team onto the field prior to the start of all home football games. After the coin toss at midfield, Chief Osceola, holding a 10-foot flaming spear over his head, rides Renegade from the far end zone of the stadium to mid-field where the huge Seminole head is painted. Renegade rears up on his hind legs, and Chief Osceola plants the fiery spear into the turf. Chief Osceola and Renegade were the brain-child of head football coach Bobby Bowden's wife, Anne.

DICKSON STREET BANANA NUT BREAD
ARKANSAS RAZORBACK

2 1/2 cups sifted all-purpose flour
3 teaspoons baking powder
1/2 teaspoon salt
1 cup sugar
1/4 cup soft margarine or butter
1 egg, beaten
3 ripe bananas, mashed
1 tablespoon grated orange peel
1/2 cup milk
1/2 cup chopped pecans

Preheat oven to 350 degrees. Mix flour with baking powder and salt. Set aside. In medium bowl beat (with wooden spoon or mixer) sugar, butter, and egg until smooth. Add bananas, orange peel, and milk, mixing well. Stir in pecans. Pour batter into greased 9 x 5 x 3 inch loaf pan and bake for 1 hour. Let cool and cut into thin slices.

BIG AL

In the 1960s, the first Big Al took part in games, although the mascot wasn't legitimized until 1979, when it was voted upon by students. Students try out each season to win the coveted Big Al title.

Fans and students have attempted to change the mascot to make it more compatible with the nickname. The mythological figure Trident was tried once, as was a simple wave; however, they never were popular.

DINNER ROLLS
ALABAMA CRIMSON TIDE

4 to 4 1/2 cups all purpose flour
1 package active dry yeast
1 cup milk
1/3 cup sugar
1/3 cup butter, margarine or shortening
1 teaspoon salt
2 eggs

In large bowl, combine 2 cups flour and yeast. In saucepan, heat milk, sugar, butter, and salt just until warm (115 degrees) and butter is almost melted; stir constantly. Add flour mixture. Add eggs. Beat at low speed of electric mixer 1/2 minute, scraping sides of bowl constantly. Beat 3 minutes at high speed. Stir in as much remaining flour as you can mix with a spoon. Turn onto floured surface. Knead in enough remaining flour to make moderately stiff dough. Shape into ball. Place in a greased bowl; turn once. Cover; let rise in warm place until double in size (about 1 hour). Punch down; divide dough in half. Cover and let rest 10 minutes. Shape into desired rolls. Let rise until nearly double. Bake in 375-degree oven for 12 to 15 minutes. Makes 24 to 30 rolls.

GIANT BURGER BUN
GEORGIA BULLDOG

2 3/4 to 3 1/4 cups all purpose flour
1 cup Quaker oats (quick or old fashioned), uncooked
1/4 cup instant nonfat dry milk
2 tablespoons sugar
1 package active dry yeast
1 teaspoon salt
1 cup very warm water (115 to 120 degrees)
1/4 cup butter or margarine
1 egg, separated
1 tablespoon sesame seeds

In a large bowl, combine 1 cup flour, oats, milk, sugar, yeast, and salt; mix well. Combine water and butter, stirring, until butter is almost melted. Add water mixture and egg yolk to flour mixture. Beat at low speed on electric mixer about 30 seconds or until just blended. Beat at medium speed for 2 minutes, scraping bowl occasionally. Add 1/4 cup flour; beat at high speed about 2 minutes, scraping bowl occasionally. With wooden spoon stir in enough remaining flour to make a stiff dough. Knead on lightly floured surface for 8 to 10 minutes or until smooth and elastic. Cover and let rise 20 minutes. Shape dough into smooth ball; flatten into greased cake pan. Brush with slightly beaten egg white; sprinkle with sesame seed. Cover loosely with plastic wrap. Refrigerate for 2 to 24 hours. (Dough will double in size.) Heat oven to 350 degrees. Uncover dough; let stand at room temperature about 20 minutes. Bake at 350 degrees for 40 to 45 minutes or until golden brown. Cool 10 minutes; remove from pan. Cool completely on wire cooling rack; split in half to form top and bottom of bun. Makes 1 giant bun. *THIS WILL BE THE HIT OF YOUR NEXT TAILGATE WHEN YOU SERVE IT WITH THE GIANT CHEESEBURGER.*

GIANT CHEESEBURGER
GEORGIA BULLDOG

1 1/2 pound ground beef
3/4 cup Quaker oats (quick or old fashioned) uncooked
3/4 cup catsup
1 egg
1 teaspoon salt
4 pasteurized process American cheese slices
Lettuce leaves
Giant Burger Bun

Heat oven to 350 degrees. In medium-sized bowl, combine all ingredients except cheese, lettuce, and bun; mix well. On rack of broiler pan, shape mixture to form 8 1/2-inch diameter patty. Bake at 350 degrees for 40 to 45 minutes or until desired doneness. Arrange cheese slices over patty. Continue baking about 1 minute or until cheese is melted. Arrange lettuce leaves on bottom of GIANT BURGER BUN; top with patty. Serve with mustard, catsup, tomato slices and pickle slices, as desired. Top with bun top; cut into 12 wedges. Makes 12 servings.

BREAD STICKS
GEORGIA SOUTHERN EAGLE

1 package hot dog buns
1 teaspoon garlic salt
1 teaspoon basil
1 teaspoon parsley flakes
1 stick margarine, melted

Separate buns where already split. Cut each half in half again longways. Coat with mixture of margarine and seasonings. Place sticks on baking sheet in oven which has been pre-heated to 200 degrees. Bake 1 to 1 1/2 hours until hard and dry. Cool and store in tightly covered container.

HAM AND CHEESE TREATS
GEORGIA BULLDOG

2 sticks butter or margarine
3 tablespoons poppy seeds
3 tablespoons prepared mustard
2 tablespoons minced onion
Sliced ham
Swiss cheese
6 (6-inch) French or sourdough rolls

Split rolls lengthwise. Mix first 4 ingredients and spread rolls generously on both pieces. On bottom half, place sliced ham, then Swiss cheese. Replace top half, slice into 4 pieces cross-wise, and bake 10 minutes at 350 degrees. May be made up and kept in the refrigerator to bake as needed.

BIG RED

The University of Arkansas used the nickname Cardinals (for school colors) until 1909. An unbeaten football season that year prompted Arkansas Coach Hugo Bezdek to describe his team as "a wild band of Razorbacks." The Razorback nickname caught on, and fans added the famous battle cry, "Whooo, Pig! Sooie" during the 1920s.

Since the 1960s, Arkansas has had five different live mascots, including two duroc pigs, an Australian wild boar, and Ragner, a wild hog captured in southern Arkansas. The current porker, Big Red VI, makes rounds before the game but no longer remains in Razorback Stadium after kickoff.

TAILGATING—THE MSU TRADITION

Football is a tradition at Mississippi State. And along with football come tailgate parties. Traditionally, to have a tailgate party you had to have a truck—since you had to have a tailgate to be your table. Now, at least at MSU, a tailgate party is any get-together before a football game. To be a true tailgate party, it really should be a picnic, but we have been known to call indoor parties before a football game a tailgate party, too.

Our family has been tailgating in the same place every year, for every football game for 15 years. We have claimed the next-to-last tree on Bell Island across from the MSU Alumni House as our own. We picked that spot because it is close to the stadium and is in the middle of all the action. Anyone who walks from the student union to the cafeteria to the stadium has to walk by our tree. Because of our location, we always run into people we know. And we always invite them to eat with us.

I was only eight years old the first time I tailgated and then attended the MSU Homecoming football game. What I remember most are the sights, sounds, and smells of the campus. There were so many tailgate parties going on around us that I was overwhelmed. I remember all my parents' friends talking about the game and how well the Bulldogs had been doing that season. I also remember the enormous quantities of food on our table. I had seen that much food only on my grandmother's table at Thanksgiving. Amazingly enough, most of it was gone by the time we left to walk to the stadium.

At MSU we think that the best food for a tailgate party is finger food like sandwiches, fried chicken, cookies, chips, and other snack foods. We have smoked meat and rolls with home-made Bully's Barbecue Sauce, Dawg Bites with sweet and sour dipping sauce, MSU Mint Chocolate Brownies, and Every Bulldog's Favorite Chocolate Chip Cookies. We usually have a tray with different snack foods like Puppy Chow, candy corn, jelly beans, and crackers. Pasta salad, chips and dip, and cheese balls (made from MSU cheese, of course) round out our tailgate parties.

And we always bring an ice chest full of drinks, especially for those games early in the season when the weather is warm. For true Southern tailgaters, iced tea is a must. We save old single-serving fruit juice bottles, rinse them out, and fill them with sweet tea for a cooling drink at hot tailgate parties. For the colder days, we bring a Thermos bottle of coffee, Rushing Yards Spice Tea, or hot chocolate.

—*Denise McDonald, Mississippi State*

REBEL PRIDE

Florida played the "Yankee" team Penn State in 1962. To demonstrate regional pride, the Gator players placed decals of Confederate flags on their helmets.

DESERTED

When Red Sanders coached at Vanderbilt in the 1940s, he commented that "the only thing worse than finishing second is to be lying on the desert alone with your back broken. Either way, nobody ever finds out about you."

VANDERBILT'S EARLY GLORY

Vanderbilt's football history goes back over a hundred years. In November 1890, Peabody Normal College challenged Vanderbilt to a football game on Thanksgiving Day. Dr. William L. Dudley, president of the Vanderbilt Athletic Association and chemistry professor, called a mass meeting of students to the gymnasium. A motion was made and passed unanimously that Elliott Jones, a student from Kansas City who had seen some Harvard football games, organize a team and serve as its captain and coach. Jones rounded up 13 players—11 starters and two subs. Vanderbilt players wore padded breeches, long stockings, tightly-laced sleeved canvas jackets, and hockey caps. The game was played at Sulphur Dell, the city's professional baseball field; Vanderbilt won, 40-0. Vanderbilt players soon became campus heroes. Elliott Jones agreed to remain captain and coach, and by September 1891, four games had been scheduled with Sewanee and Washington University. The only loss of the 1891 season was to Washington University, 24-6.

Dr. William Dudley, Dean of the School of Medicine, organized the Southern Intercollegiate Athletic Association in 1893 and served as president until his death in 1914. Vanderbilt's Dudley Field is named in his honor.

Dan McGugin became Vanderbilt coach in 1904; he would coach at the University for 30 years. His first team scored a total of 196 points in its first three games, shutting out Mississippi A&M, Georgetown, and Ole Miss. For the entire 1904 season, 452 points were scored against eight opponents' four points!

First Quarter Drive

3

Sandwiches

NOTES

❧ 3 ❧

Sandwiches

A tailgater's standby is sandwiches. Whether they are eaten as quick snacks or the main part of a meal, sandwiches are a "must" for game days.

PIMENTO CHEESE SPREAD
MISSISSIPPI STATE BULLDOG

1 pound Mississippi State Cheddar Cheese, grated (available from the MSU Dairy Science Dept.)
2 medium-size jars of diced pimento peppers
1 tablespoon sour cream
3 tablespoons mayonnaise
Garlic powder
Pepper

Mix together for sandwiches before or after the game!

FOOTBALL PIMENTO CHEESE
SOUTH CAROLINA GAMECOCK

1 (16-ounce) package of Kraft medium, sharp cheese
7 ounces sweet relish
5 boiled eggs
1 tablespoon sugar
1 (7-ounce) jar sliced pimento
1/4 to 1 1/2 cup Dukes mayonnaise

Grate cheese and sprinkle with sugar. Mash eggs and mix in pimento and pickle relish. Add to cheese. Add mayonnaise.

Mixture will be soupy. Must be refrigerated for 24 hours. Will keep 6 weeks in refrigerator.

BULLDOG BITES
GEORGIA BULLDOG

Loaf of French bread
Italian dressing
Cheddar cheese
Your choice of cheese
Deli meat (ham, turkey, etc.)

Preheat oven to 400 degrees. Cut a loaf of French bread in half lengthwise. Spread Italian dressing (bottled) on both halves. Put on cookie sheet and into oven and bake until browned. Slice Cheddar cheese and place on bottom half. Put bottom half back in oven until cheese almost melts. Remove and put deli meat (ham, turkey, etc.) on top of cheese. Put top half of bread over meat and cut into Bulldog bites to share at tailgate party!

HAM AND SWISS CHEESE SANDWICHES
GEORGIA TECH YELLOW JACKET

Ham
Swiss cheese
1 tablespoon poppy seed
1 tablespoon prepared mustard
1 package Pepperidge Farm party rolls
1 tablespoon minced onion
1 stick melted margarine or butter

Split party rolls (as though they are one). Spread both sides with margarine, poppy seed, mustard, and onion. Layer cheese, then ham. Cover with foil. Bake, covered, at 350 degrees for 15 minutes. Can freeze before baking.

THE REAL GAME DAY

College football, born on a windy November Saturday afternoon in 1869, has since been associated with autumn Saturdays in America.

The lure of television revenues has coaxed many big-time teams to schedule games on holidays, Thursdays, or prime-time Friday nights. But diehard fans, especially avid tailgaters with intense emotional ties to their game, know that Saturday will always be *Game Day*.

KENTUCKY WILDCAT SANDWICH
GEORGIA BULLDOG

8 slices bacon
1 tablespoon sherry or Madeira
2 tablespoons butter or margarine
3 tablespoons Parmesan cheese
2 tablespoons minced onion
4 slices ham
2 tablespoons all purpose flour
4 slices turkey or chicken
1 cup chicken broth
8 thin slices tomato
2 tablespoons Half and Half
8 slices wheat or white toast

Fry the bacon until just cooked. Keep the heat low so the fat does not smoke. Drain well. In saucepan, melt the butter. Saute the onion until soft. Stir in the flour. Cook for 2 minutes. Slowly stir in the broth, using a whisk to combine well. Cook until thickened, Lower heat. Add cream, sherry or Madeira, and cheese. Keep warm. Toast the bread and butter. Place ham and turkey on 4 slices. Top with tomato slices. Spoon as much sauce as desired on each sandwich. Top with bacon. Serve at once. Or top with toast. Place on baking sheet. Heat 5 minutes at 400 degrees. Serve.

GEORGIA PARADE

In Athens, Georgia Coach Ray Goff, who replaced Vince Dooley in 1989, created a new tradition by having his football players walk past fans and tailgaters as they enter Sanford Stadium for pregame warmups.

Later, the famous Redcoat Band and Georgettes march in

quick-step under the bridge and into the stadium, pumping the already fired-up fans into a pregame frenzy.

Walking across old north campus, the Bulldog cheerleaders head toward the stadium singing Georgia cheers. They often stop near the brick Fine Arts Building to execute a rousing routine to the delight of tailgaters milling around their cars. Nearby, laughing children slide down a big hill on cardboard boxes above Georgia's student bookstore parking lot.

Tailgate picnicking creates a haven for people watching. All kinds of interesting people walk past: youngsters selling game programs and out-of-town visitors looking lost; lovely young belles hoping to be noticed; and grizzled old-timers thinking only of what they're hearing inside the headphones mounted to their ears.

Add the lively music, hot grilled foods and crisp, cool breezes, and it's easy to see why Georgia fans, like people everywhere, love the great American outdoor festivals called tailgating.

SOUTH CAROLINA GAMECOCK SUB SANDWICH or THE BOWERS BOYS' SPECIAL
SOUTH CAROLINA GAMECOCK

2 loaves French bread, sliced lengthwise
Ham slices
Chicken slices
Mayonnaise
Gulden's mustard
Lettuce
Tomato slices
Onion slices
Dill pickle juice
Salt
Pepper
Nature's seasoning

Spread top slice of bread with mayonnaise and bottom with Gulden's mustard. Layer ham slices and chicken slices. Add lettuce, tomato, and onion slices. Sprinkle with a little dill pickle juice. Add salt, pepper, and Nature's seasoning. Slice into small pieces.

PILE 'EM UP SANDWICHES
GEORGIA BULLDOG

For spreading on bread:
French bread
Mustard
Garlic butter
Mayonnaise with curry powder

In ice chest:
Swiss cheese
Baked ham
Tomatoes
Cucumber
Lettuce
Olives
Pickles

Wrap individual (miniature) French loaves to carry to tailgate. Take along prepared mustard, garlic butter, and/or mayonnaise with curry powder for spreading on split loaves of bread. In ice chest, take baked ham, Swiss cheese, tomatoes, cucumber (to be sliced at tailgate). Also take lettuce, olives, pickles—whatever you like. *Let everyone stack up a hero sandwich!*

CHICKEN IN A BISCUIT
SOUTH CAROLINA GAMECOCK

2 cups chopped chicken
3 ounces cream cheese
2 tablespoons chopped pimento
2 tablespoons chopped onion
2 tablespoons milk
1/4 cup Italian bread crumbs
1 package (8) crescent rolls
1/4 cup melted butter
Salt and pepper

Combine chicken, cream cheese, pimento, milk, onion, and salt and pepper to taste. Open crescent rolls and lay flat. Place about 2 tablespoons of mixture in crescent roll. Fold edges of roll over chicken. Brush tops of filled crescent rolls with melted butter and sprinkle with Italian bread crumbs. Bake at 350 degrees for 25 minutes, or until golden brown. Makes 8.

RAZORBACK SAUSAGE HOAGIES
MISSISSIPPI REBEL

1 pound Italian sausage, cut into lengths
1 large Vidalia onion, thinly sliced
2 to 4 tablespoons asparagus beef soup (optional)
4 tablespoons prepared mustard
4 individual-sized loaves French bread

Put the sausage in a skillet and cook over medium heat until cooked through, about 10 minutes. Prick the sausages to release some juices. Add the Vidalia onion and (optional) soup and saute in the pan juices about 5 to 10 minutes. Cut each loaf of bread almost completely through and spread with mustard. Fill with sausages and onions and serve.

GUMBO BURGERS
LOUISIANA STATE TIGER

1 pound hamburger
1 can chicken gumbo soup
Hamburger buns

Brown 1 pound hamburger (scrambled) and drain. Pour in 1 can chicken gumbo soup. Heat. Serve on hamburger buns. *This is good with mustard.*

LEGION FIELD LEGEND

Auburn and Alabama fans have turned tailgating into a fine art. Parties and cookouts surface everywhere before the annual Iron Bowl showdown in Birmingham, which in some years migrates to the Plains.

Sometimes the foods outside Legion Field, too tempting to

pass up, even unite warring parties—those separate camps pledging allegiance to orange or crimson...if only until the opening kickoff.

Everywhere you turn, fans are eating and drinking, many standing outside cars, vans, and RVs scripted with "Roll Tide" or "War Eagle" on rear windows. Small-time entrepreneurs do a brisk business hawking aromatic barbecue from their front yard.

And like the world-famous Georgia-Florida tailgate party in Jacksonville, described as "one of the great spectacles in sport," hundreds of Alabamians host intimate cocktail parties around Legion Field.

CROCKPOT SANDWICHES
MISSISSIPPI STATE BULLDOG

Homemade rolls or biscuits
Ham, fried
Smoked sausage
Peanut butter
Jelly

Fill a crockpot with homemade rolls or biscuits. Just before the tailgate party, split the rolls and fill with fried ham, smoked sausage, or peanut butter and jelly. Heat them in the crock pot until warm. Leave the top on, and they should stay warm for quite a while. Serve with orange juice on a warm day or with coffee when the weather is cold.

HAM AND ASPARAGUS ROLLUPS
GEORGIA TECH YELLOW JACKET

2 slices boiled or baked ham per serving
1 tablespoon salt
Green asparagus spears
1 cup grated cheese
Cheese sauce (enough to serve 10 to 12)
4 tablespoons butter or margarine
2 cups milk

Melt butter, add flour, and blend well. Add milk and salt. Cook until slightly thickened. Add cheese, and heat until melted.

Place 3 or 4 asparagus spears on ham slices. Roll up and fasten with toothpick. Place rolls side by side in baking dish and pour 2 or 3 tablespoons of cheese sauce over each roll. Bake at 275 degrees for about 20 minutes. Serve on crisp toast.

MEXICAN ROLLUPS
GEORGIA BULLDOG

1 (8-ounce) package cream cheese
Garlic powder, to taste
1 (4-ounce) can black olives
Flour tortillas
1 (4-ounce)can chopped green chiles
1 (14-ounce) jar picante sauce

Combine cream cheese, olives, chiles, and 1 teaspoon picante sauce. Spread on flour tortillas. Roll up. Refrigerate at least 1 hour. Slice in 3/4" slices. Insert toothpick and dip in picante sauce.

THE RUN

At Clemson University's Memorial Stadium, more popularly called Death Valley, orange is dominant, from the giant paws leading into this South Carolina village to the orange carpet and walls in the Luxury boxes.

Fans love eating outdoors at Clemson, including hundreds who sail across Lake Hartwell to dock within view of the mammoth arena. Traditional fried chicken is a local favorite.

But in the heart of Orange Territory is a blue carpet laid across a slight rise at one end of Death Valley. And near the top of that hill rests a sacred rock. Clemson players enter the field for the opening kickoff by touching the rock and running down the carpet onto the playing field.

"The Run," as the pregame ritual is known, is meant for good luck and to intimidate visiting teams. As Atlanta sports columnist Furman Bishop observed, "I'm waiting for the day some guy falls and a whole pack of Tigers come sprawling down after him."

🍴

Second-Quarter Domination

4

Salads

NOTES

❧ 4 ❧

Salads

Gone are the days when a salad consisted of a head of lettuce and a few vegetables. Pasta, chicken, shrimp, and Mexican—today's salads can make a complete meal or serve as the delicious prelude to the main course.

A Clemson fan shared a trick for packing a salad for a picnic. Fit a small water-tight container into a larger one. Weight down the inner container. Fill the outer container with water and freeze. On Game Day, place your salad in the inner container, cover, and leave for the stadium. Cabbage stays freshest the longest.

CHICKEN SALAD
GEORGIA BULLDOG

2 cups cut up chicken
Salt and pepper, to taste
1 cup cut up celery
2 or 3 hard boiled eggs
1 tablespoon lemon juice
1/2 cup mayonnaise, folded in

Combine all ingredients. If desired, add pickles or relish to taste.

FOOTBALL AND FOOD #1

All roads seem to lead to college campuses in the fall. It doesn't matter where you live. People everywhere enjoy eating outdoors. And Americans love football.

In a national poll taken in 1991, Americans rated football as their favorite spectator sport.

Professional football topped the 10 most popular spectator sports, followed closely by college football. Even high school football ranked sixth, above both NBA basketball and figure skating.

Perhaps nowhere in the country is that love for cooking outdoors better paired with an unbridled affection for the game of football than in the South.

CHICKEN SALAD WITH GRAPES
GEORGIA TECH YELLOW JACKET

4 cups chicken, cooked and diced
1/2 cup sour cream (non-fat plain yogurt, if desired)
1/2 cup chopped celery
2 cups seedless grapes
1/2 teaspoon Dijon mustard
1/2 cup mayonnaise or Miracle Whip (lite, if desired)
Toasted, slivered almonds
Salt and pepper, to taste

Combine all ingredients. Chill until ready to serve.

MARINATED SHRIMP AND PASTA SALAD
GEORGIA BULLDOG

2 cups uncooked elbow or shell macaroni
1 (4 1/2 ounce) can medium shrimp, drained, rinsed, and soaked, as label directs
1/2 cup vegetable oil
1/2 cup lemon juice
1 (7-ounce) package Italian dressing mix
1 1/2 cup shredded carrots
1 1/2 cup sliced Zucchini
1/4 cup chopped green onions

Cook macaroni as package directs. Rinse and drain. In a small jar with lid or cruet, combine oil, lemon juice, and salad dressing mix. Shake well. In a large bowl, combine all other ingredients. Toss with dressing; cover and chill several hours or overnight, stirring occasionally. Refrigerate leftovers. Makes 8 to 10 servings. Add 1/4 cup pimento to make it a "DAWG" salad.

MEXICAN SALAD
AUBURN TIGER

1 small chopped onion
1 medium bag tortilla chips
4 small chopped tomatoes
1 large avocado, sliced
1 head lettuce
1 pound ground beef
1 (8-ounce) package of grated Cheddar cheese
1 (15-ounce) can kidney beans
1 (16-ounce) bottle Thousand Island dressing
1/4 teaspoon salt

Brown ground beef and drain. Add kidney beans (drained) and salt. Simmer about 10 minutes. Let cool. Break up head of lettuce and toss with onion, tomatoes, and grated cheese. Then toss with dressing. Crunch up; add tortilla chips and avocado. Toss meat and salad mixture. Serves 8. When tailgating, take meat and salad mixture separately. Mix when time to eat.

UNIVERSAL TAILGATING

Tailgating is popular nationwide. Where people gather early for an outdoor sporting event, you can bet that food is nearby.

Why is tailgating so universally embraced? People get hungry. They like to socialize. Tailgaters can avoid the rush of traffic. They sit and relax. That's also why tailgating is popular after games: good food, less traffic.

When the Sacramento Gold Miners of the Canadian Football League opened their initial season in California, *Sacramento Bee* columnist R.E. Graswich noted that, "Happy and hopeful fans turned out in force to toast the team's start at pregame tailgate parties." Some CFL fans arrived as early as 9 a.m., preparing barbecues, tossing Nerf footballs, and mingling around the parking lot.

Rich Amico, a Buffalo Bills season ticket holder, was married on opening Game Day in 1991 next to a dumpster in the parking lot at Rich Stadium in Orchard Park, New York, Amico's family and friends always park and tailgate next to the dumpster, which they decorate with Bill banners and signs.

In Camden, South Carolina, more than 60,000 horse racing fans converge to tailgate and party at two National Steeplechase Association events: the Carolina Cup and the Colonial Cup.

Tailgaters line the Springdale Race Course fence line and around the infield. A tailgate picnic competition yields spreads ranging from smoked turkey, prime rib, shrimp and oysters on the half shell to scotch eggs, salmon, and pheasant.

The fall Colonial Cup races, spaced about 30 minutes apart, offer a pleasant diversion between more rounds of tailgating and socializing with friends who drop by. At the springtime Carolina Cup, which draws a college-age crowd, picnics are likely to include sandwiches, salsa, and a seemingly endless supply of beer.

The spectator sport of Polo, such as that played in Palm Beach, has been making a comeback in recent years. The polo picnic, described as "the summer equivalent of the football tailgate," is a formal and planned affair often featuring cheeses, fruit, sweet biscuits, chilled soup, Champagne.

Another polo picnic favorite is Pimm's Cup, an English liquor served in a tall glass over ice with a cucumber peel and slice of lemon and topped with a citrus-flavored soda.

At Colorado Rockies baseball games, fans drive from as far away as Nebraska and Montana to tailgate in the parking lot outside Mile High Stadium before filling the arena to capacity and stomping their feet in excitement.

On the eastern slopes of Leadville, Colorado, fans and tourists gather along a dirt road between the old Ibex mine and Resurrection No. 2 for the 22-mile Leadville International Pack Burro Race.

Once each year, on Boom Days Sunday, dozens of spectators unfold lawn chairs and spread tailgates with snacks to look across the Arkansas River Valley waiting for the runners and pack-burros to pass.

To promote its summer reading program, the San Francisco Public Library in 1993 awarded children who read eight books with tickets to a Giants-Padres baseball game and a pre-game tailgate party with a chance to meet players.

In suburban Boston, construction company owner Ken Wexton, 51, still loves rock-and-roll. Before big shows, he hires a van and a driver and indulges in food and drink at a pre-concert tailgate party.

In 1993, Wisconsin clinched the Big Ten title and a trip to the Rose Bowl after beating Michigan State in the Tokyo Dome in Japan. About 300 Badger fans joined a Japanese crowd of 51,500 after grilling bratwurst at a Wisconsin pregame tailgate party.

SPAGHETTI SALAD
GEORGIA BULLDOG

1 (12-ounce) package of spaghetti
2 tablespoons lemon juice
3 tablespoons Accent seasoning
1 teaspoon salt
1 tablespoon garlic salt
1/4 cup oil
1 large can black olives
1 jar pimento
4 green onions
1 tablespoon mayonnaise
Salt
Pepper

Break spaghetti into pieces. Cook and drain. Mix lemon juice, seasonings, and oil into spaghetti. Store in refrigerator for 24 hours. Mix olives, pimento, and onions together; add mayonnaise and salt and pepper to taste. Combine with spaghetti mixture and store in refrigerator. It gets better after it stays in the refrigerator a couple of days.

A TECH-STYLE PREGAME BASH

At Georgia Tech's Atlanta urban campus, a really big game can turn Bobby Dodd Way north of the stadium into a street festival.

Food vendors, marching bands, corporate tents, and radio talk shows create a festive setting for thousands of excited fans sporting blue and gold. Some students plop down of the sidewalk for pregame snacking.

In 1994, Tech officials began a campaign to return the engineering school's older traditions, such as allowing Tech students onto Grant Field before the game to welcome the Yellow Jacket team. In recent years, the team entered the field through a tunnel and blasts of smoke.

Officials even reinstituted a half-time fireworks show that was tried in the late 1980s.

PEPPER MEDLEY
GEORGIA BULLDOG

6 large peppers
3 tablespoons chopped fresh basil or 1 1/2 teaspoon dried basil
3 tablespoons olive oil
2 tablespoons wine vinegar
1/4 teaspoon freshly ground pepper
3 cloves garlic, peeled

Wash peppers and cut into lengthwise sections. Discard seeds and inner core. Cut peppers into lengthwise strips approximately 1 1/2-inch long. Cut strips in half. In a 10-inch skillet, cook olive oil, red wine vinegar and garlic cloves on medium-high until garlic turns light brown. Discard garlic, add peppers, and increase heat to high. Cook peppers over high heat for 8 minutes. Add basil and pepper and cook 2 additional minutes. Peppers may be served as a side dish or with cooked pasta and freshly grated Parmesan cheese. Delicious served cold fresh from the cooler. Serves 6.

MSU ALUMNI ANTIPASTA
MISSISSIPPI STATE BULLDOG

2 (4-ounce) cans mushrooms, cut and drained
1 (14-ounce) can artichoke hearts, cut and drained
1 small jar stuffed olives, cut and drained
1 small jar pimentos, chopped and drained
1 can black olives, chopped and drained
1/4 cup chopped bell pepper
1/4 cup chopped celery

Mix all ingredients together.

Dressing

2/3 cup white vinegar
2/3 cup olive oil
1/4 cup minced dry onion
1 1/2 teaspoon Italian seasoning
1 teaspoon salt
1 teaspoon garlic salt
1 teaspoon onion salt
1 teaspoon seasoned salt
1/2 teaspoon seasoned pepper
1 teaspoon sugar
1 teaspoon Accent

Mix ingredients together and bring to a boil. Let cool. Pour over chopped ingredients. Cool. Serve with crackers or chips.

SUGAR BOWL BOUND SALAD
ALABAMA CRIMSON TIDE

1 head of lettuce
1 cucumber
1 bottle Italian dressing
1 tomato
1 package frozen English peas
1/2 cup grated cheese
1 onion
2 to 6 boiled eggs
1 green pepper
1/2 pound bacon (fried or crumbled) or bacon bits
3 stalks celery
2 1/2 cups mayonnaise
1/2 cup olives

First (bottom) layer: shredded lettuce. *Second layer*: Combined chopped onion, celery, olives, cucumber, and pepper. *Third layer*: English peas, cheese and mayonnaise. Let set overnight. Also marinate tomato in 1/2 cup oil and vinegar. Just before serving, add tomatoes and remainder of dressing. Top with bacon bits and eggs.

TAILGATE POTATO SALAD
AUBURN TIGER

8 to 10 potatoes peeled and boiled
1 medium onion, chopped
4 hard cooked eggs
3/4 cup diced celery
1 bell pepper
4 to 6 slices fried bacon, crumbled
3 tablespoons bacon grease
1 tablespoon garlic salt
1/2 tablespoon pepper
1/2 tablespoon celery salt
1/2 tablespoon paprika
1/4 cup mayonnaise
1 cup sour cream

Mix all ingredients together and promptly refrigerate. Great served hot or cold. Keeps up to 1 week in the refrigerator.

THE FIRST WAR EAGLE

The first War Eagle, according to Auburn legend, was found wounded at the Battle of the Wilderness in Virginia in 1864. A young Confederate soldier nursed the bird to health and brought it home to Auburn, where the soldier joined the faculty after the war.

During the 1892 game against Georgia at Atlanta's Piedmont Park, the old eagle, legend says, broke free from its master and soared above the field when Auburn scored the first touchdown.

Auburn faithful looked skyward and shouted, "War Eagle!" Auburn won, 10-0, and afterward the eagle collapsed and died.

The most accepted story behind the origin of the mascot hails from the 1913 football season, as the team prepared for a game against Georgia. At a pep rally, an Auburn cheerleader told the crowd, "If we are going to win this game, we'll have to get out there and fight, because this means war." During the excitement, a student, E.T. Enslen, dressed in his military uniform, lost the metal eagle emblem from his hat. When another student asked him what it was, he loudly answered, "It's a War Eagle!" Other students and fans heard him, and the cry, "Waaaaaar Eagle!" was used at the football game the next day. Today, War Eagle V (also known as Tiger) is the school's live mascot; he lives in a specially designed aviary next to Jordan-Hare Stadium.

TEXAS BEAN SALAD
GEORGIA BULLDOG

1 can red kidney beans
1/2 cup stuffed olives, sliced
1 can whole green beans
1 (2-ounce) can pimentos, diced
1 can yellow wax beans
1/2 cup salad oil
1 can garbanzo beans
1/2 cup white vinegar
1 green pepper, cut into strips
1/2 cup sugar
1 red pepper, cut into rings

Mix vegetables. Combine salad oil, vinegar, and sugar in a covered jar. Shake well. Pour over bean mixture. Cover and marinate at least 6 hours before serving. Makes 10 servings.

BAMA "QB KEEPER" SALAD
ALABAMA CRIMSON TIDE

1 pound macaroni shells
1 cup diced ham
1 cup diced provolone cheese
1 cup diced Swiss cheese
1/2 cup chopped onions
1 cup chopped celery
1 cup chopped green peppers
1 can small pitted ripe olives
1 bottle Italian salad dressing (with olive oil is best)
Salt and pepper to taste

Cook macaroni as directed. Add all other ingredients. Toss and chill at least 1 hour before leaving for the game.

CORN SALAD
MISSISSIPPI STATE BULLDOG

2 cans Shoe Peg Corn (drained)
1/2 cup chopped green onions
2 ripe tomatoes (diced)
Jalapeno peppers, chopped (to taste)
1 teaspoon Lemon Pepper seasoning
4 tablespoons mayonnaise

Mix all ingredients and refrigerate overnight. Good served with Triscuit crackers.

"N0. 1" FINGER SALAD
ALABAMA CRIMSON TIDE

Crust:
Use 2 cans crescent rolls

Filling:
2 (8-ounce) packages cream cheese
1 cup salad dressing
1 package original Ranch dressing

Top:
1/2 bunch broccoli
1/2 head cauliflower
1 carrot
1/2 onion
1 stalk celery
Tomatoes (optional)
Olives (optional)
Cucumbers (optional)

Press crescent rolls in bottom of pan. Bake until brown. Mix together filling and pour on top. Grate carrot, onion, and celery.

Sprinkle on top. Cut 1/2 head of broccoli and cauliflower. Press into filling. Let cool for 30 minutes.

STARS FELL OVER ALABAMA BLT SALAD
ALABAMA CRIMSON TIDE

8 slices bacon, cut into 1/2-inch pieces
2 cups each packed spinach leaves and torn Bibb lettuce
1 1/2 cups shredded Monterey Jack cheese
1 small thinly sliced onion, separated into rings
3 seeded and coarsely chopped plum tomatoes
1/4 cup red wine vinegar
1 teaspoon brown sugar
1/4 teaspoon salt
1/8 teaspoon freshly ground black pepper
1/2 cup prepared croutons

Cook bacon in a 10-inch skillet until crisp. Drain on paper towels. Pour off and discard all but three tablespoons drippings. Combine lettuce, spinach, Monterey Jack cheese, onion rings, and tomato. In a small bowl combine vinegar, sugar, salt, and pepper. Add to drippings in skillet. Heat to a boil, stirring constantly. Sprinkle with croutons and crisp bacon. Serves 6.

THE BEAR

How did "The Bear" earn his nickname? According to biographies, Paul Bryant was a 12-year-old farm boy living near Fordyce, in southern Arkansas, when friends convinced him to wrestle a brown bear that was at a local theater as part of a traveling sideshow.

The muzzled bear reared up. Bryant attacked it, knocking it to the ground. He held on tightly, because for every minute he wrestled the bear, the bear's handler had promised to pay him a dollar. A dollar per minute was huge money in the summer of 1926—a time when people earned 50 cents a day picking cotton.

As Bryant held on, the handler became agitated and upset the bear. The animal jerked violently and freed itself. It shook off its muzzle and bit Bryant's right ear. Bryant fled and crashed into theater seats. The chair collision scarred his legs.

After Bryant ran, the bear handler left with his animal without paying Bryant for his time on stage. The only thing Bryant earned that day was a nickname that became associated with one of college football's greatest coaches.

Several years after the wrestling match, Bryant traveled to Fayetteville, Arkansas, with Don Hutson, a University of Alabama football star. The two men happened upon a carnival sideshow.

Bryant, by then an Alabama assistant football coach, was amazed to find the bear handler and the same bear he wrestled more than a decade earlier.

Coach Bryant resisted the temptation to confront the aging bear handler about the money he never received as a boy. He said he believed the man undoubtedly needed the money more than he did.

WHO'S WHO?

In the early 1950s, two Southeastern Conference coaches tried an innovative, and short-lived, jersey numbering system. At Kentucky, coach Paul "Bear" Bryant identified twins Harry and Larry Jones, who both lettered three years (1950-52) with the numbers 1A and 1B.

At LSU, Coach Gaynell "Gus" Tinsley in 1952 used a numbering system that abbreviated a player's position on his jersey. Quarterbacks, left halfbacks, right halfbacks, fullbacks, and centers wore "Q," "L," "R," "F," and "C," followed by single digit numbers. Ends, guards, and tackles wore "E," "G," and "T," followed by a single digit. The left side of the line wore odd numbers, and the right side wore even numbers.

UGA

A goat served as mascot at Georgia's first football game. UGA I, the first in a prestigious line of white English bulldogs, was named official mascot at the university in 1956. UGA I and his heirs are buried at Sanford Stadium.

🍴

5

Soups
and
Stews

❦ 5 ❦

Soups and Stews

Crisp October and November Saturdays are perfect times for soups and stews. Savored slowly or eaten heartily, they provide nourishment for both the body and spirit.

ALABAMA RED ELEPHANT STEW
AUBURN TIGER

1 medium-sized elephant
2 rabbits
Salt, pepper, garlic

Cut elephant into bite-sized pieces. Add enough brown gravy to cover. Cook over kerosene fire for 4 weeks at 460 degrees. Add salt, pepper, garlic, and rabbits to taste. Serves 3,800 people.

BEER CHEESE SOUP
GEORGIA BULLDOG

1 small onion
1/4 cup margarine or butter
1/3 cup all purpose flour
3 1/2 cup milk
1 (8-ounce) jar pasteurized process cheese spread
1 cup shredded Cheddar cheese (about 4 ounces)
1 cup beer

Cover and microwave onion and margarine in 2-quart casserole on high until onion is tender, 3 to 4 minutes. Stir in flour and bouillon, then gradually stir in milk. Cover and microwave until hot and bubbly and cheese is melted, 3 to 4 minutes; stir. Makes 5 to 6 servings. *Great for a cool football day!*

FRESH GARDEN GAZPACHO SOUP
GEORGIA BULLDOG

3 medium-size ripe tomatoes
1 medium red pepper, cut into thin strips
1 (13-ounce) can chicken broth
1 small onion, cut into thin wedges
1/2 cup Kraft free Italian dressing
2 tablespoons chopped parsley
1/2 cup dry white wine
2 cloves garlic, minced
1 small zucchini, thinly sliced and halved
1 1/2 teaspoons hot pepper sauce

Peel, seed, and chop tomatoes. Place in large bowl. Stir in remaining ingredients. Cover; chill. Makes five 1-cup servings. Preparation time: 15 minutes, plus chilling.

PETER RABBIT STEW
SOUTH CAROLINA GAMECOCK

1 pound ground beef, browned
1 cup ketchup
3/4 pound bacon
1/4 cup brown sugar
1 cup chopped onion
1 tablespoon Liquid Smoke
2 (15-ounce) cans pork and beans
3 tablespoons white vinegar
1 (15-ounce) can kidney beans, drained
1 teaspoon salt
1 (15-ounce) can butter beans
Dash pepper

Brown and drain ground beef. Put into crock pot. Brown bacon and onion and drain. Add bacon, onion, and remaining ingredients to crock pot. Stir well. Cover and cook on low 4 to 9 hours.

When ready to leave for game, unplug crock pot, wrap in news-paper, paper bag, etc., to keep warm. *Cold weather brings out this stew. Why this name is a mystery! Cooking hint: You may substitute Clemson Tiger meat for the ground beef!"*

TRADITIONS SOMETIMES CHANGE

Mike Childs, a deep-seeded Auburn fan who lives near Five Points in Athens, Georgia, understands life on the eastern Alabama Plains as well as anyone.

Tiger athletic director David Housel once described Childs, raised in Auburn, as "a 'War Eagle' in the Heart of Bulldog Country."

"Keep up the good 'Missionary Work,'" Housel wrote to Childs.

In most college towns, even the most beloved traditions sometimes pass into memory. The "conqueror" often carries a banner of progress or growth.

Childs, a news editor at the *Athens Banner-Herald*, remembers a favorite Auburn landmark that experienced major changes in 1994:

I suppose it was inevitable. Life is full of changes. Deal with it.

Progress will always be a double edged sword. But earlier this year, that sword slashed close to home. It cut a huge, wide swath through the happy memories of my youth in a sleepy, little east Alabama college town.

That little dairy diner which had the white fluorescent sign that proclaimed it the Sani-Freeze, but was more commonly and fondly referred to by patrons as the "Sani-Flush" has been forced to close.

A beloved Auburn culinary landmark for 33 years, it stood second only to the historic Toomer's Drug Store as a place with which college students and townsfolk alike identified.

For many Auburnites, a chocolate-dipped cone at The Flush was as much an Auburn tradition as a freshly-squeezed lemon-ade at Toomer's soda fountain.

Owner Bennie Hunt and his son, Butch, opened the Dairy Queen-like operation in 1961 before their were any Burger Kings or McDonald's. Heck, it was even before there were any

Dairy Queens, I think.

It was not much to look at as landmarks go. The small, wooden building with its warped floors and peeling paint looked as if it had already been abandoned years before.

But I think the sagging, worn-out building with weeds growing out between the bricks of its foundation, was always part of its charm. It had character and whatever else lived there, we didn't want to know. Hence, its unappetizing name.

Then came AmSouth Bank. They had been buying up the adjacent property on that block of Glenn Avenue downtown for years, with the intention of building a branch there. When The Flush's most recent lease ran out, the bank forced them to close down and sell.

But it was not without a fight from Auburn chili dog lovers, ice cream addicts and plain old sentimentalists.

A grassroots campaign to "Save The Flush" garnered about 12,000 signatures. Despite this impressive show of support, the bank did not waver. Too much money at stake. Plans had been made. So, The Flush was shut down.

News accounts sent to me by my parents and friends reported hundreds visiting The Flush on its final afternoon and evening of business. I'm sorry I missed it.

I, too, had been a regular. As a kid, a chocolate homemade milk shake or a tart, but creamy lemon freeze at The Flush was the greatest treat imaginable. As favorite treats go, it was second only to my habit of enjoying Vanilla Cokes at Toomer's (can I get an extra squirt of vanilla in that?)

It will be missed like an old friend. After more than three decades there, the charm and character of this little hole-in-the-wall dairy delight will be missed. In its place, a brand new, sparkling state-of-the-art brick, steel, and glass bank.

Despite the sadness of losing the original Flush, all the news from the Loveliest Village On The Plain is not bad.

The Hunts plan to re-open the Sani-Freeze in a small shopping center out on South College Avenue. The family is even looking at the possibility of moving the entire front of its unique, original building with its two serving windows to the new location at a cost of $10,000.

"We'll try to maintain it the way it was, but it's going to change a little bit," said the younger Hunt. "If the bank can give us the kind of financial support that we need to move the building and get started right, we'll feel really good about it."

If all goes well, he added, the 60-cent chili dogs and 93-cent milk shakes won't be gone for good.

But, of course, it won't be quite the same. These kinds of things never are.

Like the closing of The Varsity in downtown Athens, the departure of The Flush truly signifies the end of an era to thousands of Auburn students and residents.

And doesn't it seem as we grow older, more and more of the old landmarks and hangouts we once knew and loved and even took for granted are vanishing daily from our lives?

Memories of enjoying a delicious hot fudge sundae or an upside down banana split outside The Flush under a canopy of stars on a hot summer night are now just that. Memories. That place, like others, has given way to modern conveniences and greedy businessmen.

And maybe the writer Thomas Wolfe was right. You *can never* go home. But maybe it's because we just can't find it. And just maybe, it's because in this ever-changing world of ours, home never quite looks the same.

COWBULLIES

Mississippi State long endured the outdated tag "cow college" from opponents alluding to the Starkville school's ties to agriculture.

But MSU students love their cowbells, and ring them loudly at all non-Southeastern Conference sporting events. A popular story has it that a cow wondered onto the playing field during a big win over arch-rival Ole Miss and the MSU students adopted a cowbell as a good luck charm.

Mississippi State's mascot, Bully XVI, an AKC registered English Bulldog, comes from a long line of canine mascots at the state university. The link between MSU and Bulldogs began in the early 1900s, when Mississippi A&M students celebrated a shutout win over Ole Miss by parading a bulldog puppy through the streets of Jackson.

Mississippi's most famous mascot was Bully I who died in 1939 when a campus bus ran over him. The bulldog lay in state in a glass top casket and, following a half-mile funeral procession, was buried under the player's bench on the 50-yard line at Scott Field. Even *Life* magazine covered the event.

COACH AS COUNSEL

Terry Bowden is the second attorney to be named head coach at Auburn.

Chett Wynne, the first attorney to coach Auburn, served in the Nebraska legislature before moving to Auburn from Creighton. Wynne's teams compiled a 22-15-2 record between 1930-33. His 1932 team finished 9-0-1 and won the Southern Conference.

In 1993, Bowden's first year as coach, the Tigers finished 11-0-0, but were on probation and were ineligible for a bowl game or a Southeastern Conference championship.

Each player on the 1993 team received a ring inscribed with "Best in the SEC." Auburn was the only SEC team to beat both Florida and Alabama, which met in the SEC championship game.

VICTORY SPOILS

When arch-rivals face off each year, there often is more at stake than bragging rights. Some teams play for a prized old artifact.

These trophies, displayed at a winning school's campus, are tangible reminders of victory over a rival.

Kentucky and Tennessee play for a Beer Keg. Montana battles Idaho for a Wooden Beer Stein.

Michigan State battles Indiana for a Brass Spittoon, but Virginia and VPI compete for the Tobacco Bowl.

Clemson and South Carolina fight for a Tea Cup. Florida and Florida State covet the Governor's Cup. But if Florida beats Miami, the Gators get the Seminole War Canoe.

The Mississippi State-Ole Miss winner gets the Golden Egg, but the Texas Christian-Southern Methodist victor takes home the Old Frying Pan.

The Alabama-Auburn winner receives the O.D.K. Trophy. Michigan and Michigan State play for the Paul Bunyan Trophy.

Prizes with animal connections are popular too. Iowa and Minnesota vie for a coveted pig statuette, Floyd of Rosedale. Illinois and Ohio State play for Illibuck, a wooden turtle.

Colorado and Nebraska battle for a Buffalo Head, but the

Wichita-Wichita State winner shed blood for a Dog Collar.

A famous spoil of victory is the Little Brown Jug that goes home to the winner of the Minnesota-Michigan game. Indiana and Purdue brag about their Old Oaken bucket.

Whatever the prize, most rivals hope to remain cordial after the game. That may explain the Peace Pipe (Oklahoma-Missouri) and the Peace Pact (Kansas-Kansas State).

STEWED YELLOW JACKET
or AUBURN TIGER STEW
GEORGIA BULLDOG

1 (3-pound) chicken (thighs and legs)
1 cup barbecue sauce
1 (3-pound) pork roast
1/2 teaspoon black pepper
1 can yellow cream-style corn
1 teaspoon salt
1 can yellow whole kernel corn
2 tablespoons honey or maple syrup

1 can white Shoe-Peg corn
1 tablespoon garlic salt
2 large onions, chopped
1 tablespoon Worcestershire sauce
3 cans tomatoes
1 teaspoon barbecue spice
Dash Tabasco sauce

Parboil chicken and cook in 3 quarts water until tender. Remove from water and grill over charcoal until done (reserve stock from meat). Add all remaining ingredients to stock. Allow this to simmer while meat is grilling. Place pieces of grilled meat in blender, using stock mixture as liquid, and chop on grate speed. Continue this until all meat has been grated. Add meat to other ingredients. Cook slowly for approximately 4 to 6 hours. Makes 1 1/2 gallons. The longer this cooks the better, so flavor can mix. Stir often. *Cliff Davis of Gwinnett County, Georgia, always serves this at the last Georgia home game of the year.*

SEC CHAMP STEW
ALABAMA CRIMSON TIDE

1 1/2 pounds stew beef, cut into small pieces
1 medium onion, diced
5 carrots, sliced
5 potatoes, sliced
1 cup chopped celery, if desired
Salt and pepper, to taste
2 tablespoons sugar
2 tablespoons cornstarch
2 (12-ounce) cans V-8 juice

Put stew meat into bottom of casserole. Add layers of onion, carrots, potatoes, and celery. Add salt and pepper. Sprinkle with sugar and cornstarch. Pour V-8 juice over top. Cover and bake 3 1/2 hours at 300 degrees.

BUILD IT—THEY WILL COME

The original Dudley Field, site of today's Vanderbilt Stadium, was the first stadium erected exclusively for football in the South. The dedication game on Oct. 14, 1922, ended in a scoreless tie between Vanderbilt and national power Michigan.

The concrete-tiered horseshoe-shaped stadium seated 20,000 spectators—a Nashville showcase in the 1920s. In 1981, the original stadium, enlarged over the years to seat 34,000, was demolished (except for 12,088 metal seats) and rebuilt in nine months to seat 41,000.

BRUNSWICK STEW
GEORGIA BULLDOG

6 pounds stew beef, ground
2 quarts cut-up tomatoes
2 1/2 pounds pork roast, ground
1 pound butter
4 or 5 pounds chicken, ground
1 1/2 tablespoons black pepper
2 1/2 pounds onion, grated
1 1/2 tablespoons red pepper
1 quart cream corn
6 tablespoons salt

Cook everything until done. Stir often. Use meat broth to make consistency desired. A little vinegar is optional.

CUTE PRINCE CHARLES

From future kings to college freshmen, everyone has a favorite tale to share.

Great Britian's Prince Charles witnessed his first American football game on October 22, 1977, in Athens when Vince Dooley's Georgia team hosted Kentucky.

As a crowd neared to watch Charles enter University of Georgia President Fred Davison's box in the North Side Club Level, a drunken female Bulldog fan exclaimed, "G-a-a-wd, he's cute!" The heir to Britian's throne nodded politely and entered the box.

At halftime, Charles was introduced to Kentucky Coach Fran Curci and the Wildcats' 6-6 All-American, Art Still.

"You're a tall one, aren't you?" the Prince asked Still. Charles witnessed a 33-0 Kentucky victory.

HUNGRY DAWG CHOWDER
GEORGIA BULLDOG

2 cups diced raw potatoes
6 to 8 hot dogs, thinly sliced
1 (10-ounce) package frozen vegetables
1/4 cup flour
1/4 cup chopped onion
1/8 teaspoon pepper
1 tablespoon snipped parsley
3 cups milk
2 or 3 chicken bouillon cubes
2 tablespoons margarine
1/4 teaspoon salt

In a pan, combine potatoes, vegetables, onion, parsley, bouillon, and salt. Add 1 cup of water; then bring to a boil. Cover and boil gently for 15 to 20 minutes (until vegetables are tender). Add hot dog slices. Bring to boiling again and add flour, pepper, and milk. This will thicken the base. If too thin, add more milk. If a thicker base is desired, add more flour. Cook and stir for 2 minutes, then add butter or margarine. Top with paprika, if desired, and more butter. Serves 6.

SOUTHERN NICKNAMES

GAMECOCKS

The University of South Carolina is the only major college athletic program that uses the nickname Fighting Gamecocks. At the turn of the century, after struggling for more than a decade under numerous nicknames, the school's football team was first referred to unofficially as Game Cocks. In 1903, *The State*, Columbia's morning newspaper, shortened the name to one word.

Gamecock was an appropriate name since the state of South Carolina has long been connected with the breeding and training of fighting gamecocks. General Thomas Sumter, famed Revolutionary War guerilla fighter, was known as the Fighting Gamecock.

A gamecock is a fighting rooster known for its spirit and courage. A cock fight, which was a popular sport throughout the United States in the 19th century, would last until the death of one of the roosters. Although cock fighting is now outlawed in most states, it is still held surreptitiously in many areas.

THE CIVIL WAR TIGERS

In the fall of 1896, when LSU Coach A.W. Jeardeau's football team had a perfect 6-0-0 record, the school first adopted its nickname Tigers. Since most collegiate schools that year bore the names of ferocious animals, Tigers seemed a logical choice. The underlying reason, though, that Louisiana State University chose the nickname dates back to the Civil War.

A battalion of Confederate soldiers comprised of New Orleans Zouaves and Donaldsonville Cannoneers distinguished themselves at the Battle of Shenandoah. These rebels had been known as the fighting band of "Louisiana Tigers."

In 1955, the LSU Fourth-Quarter Ball Club called the Tigers the Fighting Tigers.

THE VOLUNTEER

The University of Tennessee's nickname is derived from the name most associated with the state. Tennessee acquired its nickname, "The Volunteer State," in the early 1800s when General Andrew Jackson mustered large armies from his home state to fight the Indians and later the British at the Battle of New Orleans. The name became even more significant in the Mexican War when Tennessee governor Aaron V. Brown issued a call for 2800 men to battle Santa Ana; some 30,000 men volunteered, including the famous Davy Crockett. The dragoon uniform worn by Tennessee regulars during the Fight for Texas Independence is still adorning the color guard at UT athletic events.

Third Quarter Comeback

6

Meats
and Main
Dishes

NOTES

❦ 6 ❦

Meats and Main Dishes

For many tailgaters, a meal is incomplete without meat. Whether ribs, hamburgers, or wings are served, they are sure to please hungry football fans.

BULLDOG RED SAUCE FOR ROAST
GEORGIA BULLDOG

1/2 cup butter
1 quart ketchup
5 cups water
1/4 bottle Worcestershire sauce
3/4 tablespoon hot sauce
1/2 tablespoon black pepper
1/2 tablespoon salt
1/2 tablespoon lemon juice
2 onions

Mix ingredients and let boil. Simmer 1 hour. Serve this with a whole sirloin cooked on smoker.

A BIG APPETITE FOR MEATS

John Madden, the colorful Fox Network TV football analyst and former Los Angeles Raiders coach, likes tailgating that's good and messy.

Madden says nothing beats grilled ribs and chicken smothered in a spicy barbecue sauce. He also says the best grilled foods drip with flavor and stain your shirt before you enter the stadium.

"A lot, a lot to eat," Madden told the *Los Angeles Times* of what is essential for an ideal tailgate. He says hearty food-stuff, and tons of it, is the first criterion for an "All-Madden Tailgate Lineup." He prefers sausages, Bratwurst, and sour-dough buns.

"I've always said that if I was a fan, I'd be a tailgater," Madden told the *Times*. "They beat traffic on the way in. They don't have to worry about finding parking places. They relax and enjoy it. Afterwards, they have a party, and they miss traffic on the way out."

GRILL'EM AT THE STADIUM STEAKS
GEORGIA BULLDOG

1/2 teaspoon instant minced onion
3 tablespoons wine vinegar
1/2 cup salad oil
1 teaspoon seasoned salt
Dash freshly ground pepper
2 teaspoons Worchestershire sauce
6 cubed round steaks
6 slices sharp processed American cheese
6 hamburger buns, toasted and buttered

Soak onion in vinegar for a few minutes. Add oil and seasonings, mixing well. Place meat in container. Pour marinade over, coating well. Cover. Let stand 1 hour. Spoon marinade two times and keep cool. Grill over hot coals about 2 minutes per side. At the last minute, lay the cheese slices on the steak. Serve on hot buns.

BULLY'S BARBEQUE SAUCE
MISSISSIPPI STATE BULLDOG

1/2 cup chopped onion
1/4 stick margarine
1/8 cup cider vinegar
3/4 cup catsup
4 tablespoons brown sugar
4 tablespoons molasses
3 tablespoons Worcestershire

2 tablespoons dry mustard
1 teaspoon salt
1/2 teaspoon paprika
1 teaspoon garlic powder
1/2 teaspoon black pepper

Sauté chopped onion in margarine. Add other ingredients and simmer for about 15 minutes. Place in a glass jar. Should be served warm. Place glass jar in a sink full of hot water to warm if you do not have a microwave. Serve with any kind of smoked meat—best with pork.

HOT AUBURN DOGS

You can prepare hot, juicy hot dogs at your tailgate even if you don't have a grill. An Auburn fan shared one technique she learned from her mom:

Preheat a wide-mouthed insulated jug by filling it with boiling water and letting it stand a few minutes. Empty the jug and refill it almost to the top with boiling water, leaving space for the hot dogs. Screw on the lid.

When the tailgaters are ready, add the hot dogs to the jug and let them heat in the water, with the lid on, for 7 to 10 minutes. Remove the hot dogs from the water with tongs.

CAJUN GATIN'

Tailgating is one of the richest traditions surrounding Louisiana State football. LSU fans roll into Baton Rouge in Recreational Vehicles, and campers are stocked with food as early as Thursday afternoon before a Saturday night home game.

After setting up camp, these fans kick back for a weekend of outdoor grilling and fun for two days before kickoff.

Many Tiger fans suggest that the attraction of night football at LSU goes beyond the cooler temperatures and the excitement created by a game played under lights. The foods cooked across campus and in parking lots bring them all back, they say.

Popular Cajun parking lot entrees include crawfish, jambalaya, boiled shrimp, and cochon-de-lait. An observer noted that "some of the finest foods in all of America are cooked on fall Saturday afternoons in the parking lot of Tiger Stadium."

COLD CONFETTI MEATLOAF
ALABAMA CRIMSON TIDE

1 tablespoon vegetable oil
3/4 cup chopped carrot
1/4 cup chopped sweet red pepper
1/4 cup chopped sweet green pepper
1 medium onion, chopped
1/4 teaspoon leaf sage, crumbled
3/4 pound ground beef
1/2 pound lean ground pork
1 egg, slightly beaten
1/3 cup prepared chili sauce
1 cup fresh bread crumbs
1/4 teaspoon salt
Dash of pepper
1/2 cup cubed Cheddar cheese

Heat oil in medium skillet over low heat. Add carrot, red and green pepper, onion, and sage. Cover and cook over very low heat for 10 minutes. Mixture should be tender, not browned. Preheat oven to 375 degrees. Lightly grease 8 1/2 x 4 x 2 5/8 loaf pan. Fold piece of aluminum foil to line sides and bottom of pan, but not the short ends. Leave a 1-inch overhang on each end. Lightly grease a large bowl. Gently stir in vegetables and cheese. Spoon into prepared pan. Pack lightly and smooth on top. Bake in preheated oven for 50 minutes or until juices run clear when pierced with a fork. Cool for 10 minutes. Grasp foil overhang and gently lift loaf from pan, allowing juices to drain back into pan. Place on plate. Refrigerate. When cooled, peel off foil. Keep refrigerated or in cooler.

DIFFERENT PLATES FOR DIFFERENT STATES

Where football fans live largely determines what and how they barbecue. Easterners cook great Philly cheese steaks, but Midwesterners prefer sausages and lots of cheeses when they tailgate.

Fans at Texas-Oklahoma games eat everything from caviar to Tex Mex chili and barbecued ribs. Southern California is where you'd likely spot hor d'oeuvres and wine on tableclothes outside a stadium.

In the Deep South, pork remains the favorite meat, but football fans in Texas and the great American West love beef. Arkansas Razorback fans wouldn't dare eat pork on Game Day.

Texans like to dry rub their beef with crushed ingredients like oregano, thyme, cayenne pepper, chili powder, or cumin. They let it stand for a while before grilling.

Tailgaters in western North Carolina like their pork grilled in a sweet ketchup-style sauce. In the eastern half of the Tarheel state, picnickers smother their pork, pulled off the bone, in a vinegar-based hot pepper sauce. Regardless if you're there tasting the Game Day pork or just passing through, the woods surrounding the University of North Carolina's stadium are lovely in October.

DOGGIE BURGERS
GEORGIA BULLDOG

2 pounds ground beef
1/2 cup bread crumbs
2 tablespoons minced onion
1 egg
Salt and pepper, to taste
1 (8-ounce) jar or can spaghetti sauce

Combine first 5 ingredients and shape into tiny balls. Place spaghetti sauce in saucepan and place meatballs in sauce. Simmer about 10 minutes. Provide toothpicks for serving. May be stored in refrigerator and heated as needed.

"ROAD KILL CAFE"

Cooter Waller knows all about pregame "happenings." He's been staging them in Thomaston, Georgia, for years.

In 1987, five years before R.E. Lee High School consolidated with Upson County, Waller began hosting a gathering of fans on the eve of R.E. Lee home games in middle Georgia.

Waller, a 1965 graduate of R.E. Lee, sees to it that no one goes hungry at the weekly fan fest, originally known as The Rebel Commission on Pregame Strategy Session.

Nowadays, before each Upson-Lee home game, Waller sets up a half-barrel grill in a parking area across from Matthews Field and grills whatever somebody decides to bring by.

Hamburgers, hot dogs, and venison are the norm, but Waller has cooked squirrel, rabbit, and snake during his pregame grillfest. It's the wild game that spawned the name "Road Kill Cafe."

While Waller cooks, former University of Alabama lineman Mickey Thrasher, sports director at Thomaston's WTGA (95.3 FM), hosts a live pregame show from the same parking lot.

"Come on by," says Waller, a Department of Transportation engineer, "and I'll cook you up some possum on the half shell."

CHERRY TOMATO MEATBALLS
TENNESSEE VOLUNTEER

1 beaten egg
1/2 teaspoon dried oregano
3/4 cup soft bread crumbs (1 slice bread)
Dash pepper
1 pound lean ground beef
1/2 cup skim milk
15 cherry tomatoes
1/4 cup finely chopped onion

Combine beaten egg, bread crumbs, milk, onion, oregano, and pepper. Add ground beef and mix well. Shape meat mixture evenly around each cherry tomato to form round meatballs. Place meatballs in a 13 x 9 x 2 baking pan. Bake at 375 degrees for 25 to 30 minutes. Makes 15 servings.

NEW MEMORIES

As a journalist, I've always accepted the basic truth that "Every person has a story."

Even the most outwardly dull person you meet probably has a history or life experience that 5,000 others might find interesting. Football fans are full of stories.

When old friends are gathered under bright fall skies—milling around a table tasting homemade breads or dipping corn chips or celery sticks into creamy spreads and salsas—the remembrances of glory from seasons past often flow like the sweet teas washing everything down.

With each passing season, I appreciate more the wisdom of my Dad's simple philosophy of life:

"Life is really just a bag of memories," says Bill Looney. "All we really do is create new memories each day, so you might as well fill yours with good ones."

—*Dean Looney*

KENTUCKY ODDITIES

Georgetown College, of Kentucky, played its entire 1897 three-game schedule against the same school, the University of Kentucky. Kentucky lists only one of those three games in its record books—a 20-4 win.

In 1900, Kentucky won a football game without ever running an offensive play. In a 12-6 win over the Louisville YMCA, Kentucky punted on first down every time it received the ball. The Louisville team eventually fumbled twice in its own end zone. Kentucky recovered both those fumbles to score two touchdowns.

Kentucky may be known as the Bluegrass state, but at Lexington's Commonwealth Stadium, the Wildcat football team begins each season playing on thick, green Bermuda. By late October, early morning frosts change the color of the Bermuda, and the Wildcats play on brown grass during November.

GEORGIA SWEET AND SOUR AUBURN PINEAPPLE MEATBALLS
GEORGIA BULLDOG

1/2 pound ground beef
1/4 cup dry bread crumbs
2 tablespoons chopped onion
1 egg
1/4 cup milk
1/2 teaspoon salt
1/4 teaspoon black pepper
1/4 teaspoon nutmeg
Butter or margarine

Combine all ingredients except butter in a bowl and mix well. Form into small meatballs. Fry meatballs a few at a time until browned and cooked through. Drain on paper towels. Set aside.

Sauce:
1 tablespoon oil
1/4 teaspoon salt
1 medium onion, chopped
1 medium red or green pepper, chopped

1/2 cup catsup
2 tablespoons vinegar
1 1/2 teaspoons cornstarch
1 (8-ounce) can pineapple chunks or crushed (reserve syrup)
2 tablespoons sherry (optional)
Chopped green onion (for garnish)

Prepare the sauce by heating oil in skillet. Add salt, onion, and green pepper. Cook until tender but not browned. Drain oil. Combine catsup and vinegar. Stir into the onion/pepper mixture. Make a paste with cornstarch and reserved pineapple syrup. Add to the vegetable mixture and cook, stirring, 3 to 5 minutes or until mixture thickens. Stir in pineapple chunks and sherry, if used. Simmer for 3 minutes. Mix in meatballs. Heat through. Transfer to serving bowl. Garnish with chopped green onion and serve.

GRECIAN MEATBALLS
TENNESSEE VOLUNTEER

4 slices bread
1 cup water
2 pounds ground beef
1 small onion, chopped
1/4 cup cracker crumbs
1/4 dried parsley
1 tablespoon salt
1/4 teaspoon celery seed
1/2 teaspoon pepper
1/2 teaspoon Accent
1/4 cup Parmesan cheese
3 eggs
1 cup flour, to roll meatballs in
8 ounces olive oil
10 to 12 ounces ketchup

Pour water over bread. Add remaining ingredients. Mix until blended. Roll small balls in flour. Pour 1/2 in Dutch oven pan and brown meatballs. Turn once. Remove balls. Take out half of oil and add 1/2 bottle of ketchup and 1 1/2 to 2 cups water. Add meatballs. Cover and simmer for 30 minutes. Serve with toothpicks.

AUBURN MISTAKES
ALABAMA CRIMSON TIDE

1 pound hot sausage
1 pound hamburger
1 pound Velveeta cheese
1 teaspoon garlic powder
1 teaspoon Worchestershire sauce
1 tablespoon oregano
2 loaves party rye

Cook ground meat and pork together until it changes color. Drain fat. Add spices. Add cheese slowly over low heat. Spread on party rye. Heat at 400 degrees for 10 minutes. These can also be frozen before cooking. They heat up easily and are great leftovers, even for breakfast.

CALLING ON DAVIS

Legendary Georgia Tech Head Coach Bobby Dodd called his undefeated 1952 team "the best football team that I ever coached." It was versatile, too.

In the first game, a 54-6 rout of The Citadel, the score was so one-sided that during the second quarter, a public address announcement summoned a freshman in the stands named Cecil Davis.

By the third quarter, Davis, a defensive back from Griffin, Georgia, was dressed in a Tech uniform and on the field. He later made an interception.

POLYNESIAN MEATBALLS
MISSISSIPPI REBEL

2 pounds lean ground beef
2 cups bread crumbs (about 4 slices)
1/2 cup milk
1 egg
1/8 teaspoon garlic salt
Salt
1/4 cup flour

1/4 cup salad oil
1 large can pineapple chunks
1 (8-ounce) can tomato sauce
2 small green peppers, cut into chunks
2 tablespoons vinegar

In large bowl, mix first 5 ingredients and 1 1/2 teaspoons salt. Shape into balls and coat with flour. Brown in hot salad oil. Discard drippings. In skillet, heat to boiling: pineapple and its liquid, tomato sauce, green peppers, vinegar, and 1 teaspoon salt. Simmer 15 minutes, stirring frequently.

ROAST ARKANSAS PORK BARBECUE
LOUISIANA STATE TIGER

1 (6-pound) fresh picnic shoulder
1 (16-ounce) can tomatoes
1/2 cup vinegar
1/3 bottle Worcestershire sauce
2 tablespoons salt
1 tablespoon sugar
2 teaspoons black pepper
2 teaspoons crushed red pepper

Trim fat from shoulder and cut meat into small pieces. Trim close to the bone. Put in 6-quart Dutch oven. Add remaining ingredients and mix well. Place bone in pot with pork. Bring to boil on medium-high heat. Cut back to medium-low or simmer for 3 to 4 hours. Stir occasionally. Cook until meat falls off bone and breaks up with a fork. Remove bone. Pour into colander. Put colander in Dutch oven. Cover and let drain. Put into serving dish.

COMING HOME

The first college football homecoming game originated at the University of Illinois in October 1910. The 5,000-plus Illinois grads who returned to campus during that first homecoming weekend were treated to a hobo parade, a stunt show, and a shutout victory over the visiting University of Chicago.

BARBECUE CUPS
GEORGIA TECH YELLOW JACKET

3/4-pound ground beef
1/2 cup barbecue sauce
2 teaspoons finely chopped onion
Dash of garlic powder
1 (10-count) package of refrigerated biscuits
2 ounces grated cheddar cheese

Brown beef and drain off grease. Stir in barbecue sauce, onion, and garlic powder. Mix well. Flatten each biscuit and press into muffin tin. Spoon beef mixture into center of each biscuit cup; then top with cheese. Bake at 400 degrees for 10 to 12 minutes, or until biscuits are lightly browned and cheese is melted. Makes 10 barbecue cups. *These go quickly!*

FRIED STEAK
AUBURN TIGER

2 pounds cubed round steak
Salt and pepper
Garlic (optional)

Cut steak into 2-inch strips. Sprinkle with salt and pepper. Dust with flour. Drop in hot oil. Let cook about 5 minutes or until meat floats to top. Place on paper towel to drain.

WHY CRIMSON TIDE?

University of Alabama football teams were tagged with various nicknames in the football program's early years: Varsity, Crimson White, and the Thin Red Line, a descriptive made popular by headline writers.

During the early 1900s, because of the football team's crimson jerseys, the University of Alabama's defensive line was referred to as the Thin Red Line. In 1911, during a driving rainstorm when Alabama was playing Smith College, a sportswriter said the players looked like a swarming Crimson Tide. Alabama's school cheer, "Roll Tide Roll," comes from the nickname.

Another story about the origin of the nickname is attributed to Hugh Roberts, a former sports editor for the *Birmingham Age Herald*. In describing the rain-soaked game between Alabama and Auburn, a heavy favorite, Roberts likened Alabama's stubborn defensive stand in the mud to a "Crimson Tide."

SAUSAGE BALLS
FLORIDA GATOR

2 cups Bisquick
2 cups grated sharp Cheddar cheese
1 pound sausage

Stir-fry sausage slightly. Drain and let cool. Mix cheese, Bisquick, and sausage. Make into balls. If needed, add a little water. Cook at 350 degrees for 20 minutes or until brown.

SAUSAGE CHEESE BALLS
GEORGIA TECH YELLOW JACKET

2 cups Bisquick
1 (8-ounce) package of sharp Cheddar cheese
1 pound hot sausage
1/3 cup margarine

Leave cheese and margarine at room temperature to soften. Grate cheese and blend all ingredients. Knead with hands to dough consistency. Form balls by rolling dough between palms of hands. Quick freeze on cookie sheet (about 5 to 10 minutes). Bake at 325 degrees for 15 to 20 minutes. Check periodically. You will know when they are done. Don't let them get too hard. They can be reheated by covering in foil.

COMMODORES

The nickname "Commodores" was first applied to Vanderbilt University athletic teams in 1897 by William E. Beard, a member of the editorial staff of the Nashville *Banner*. Beard was a quarterback on the 1892 Vanderbilt team. Commodore

Cornelius Vanderbilt (1794-1877) was an American steamship and railroad magnate who was popularly known as Commodore. He gave a million dollars to found Vanderbilt University in 1873.

SWEET AND SOUR SAUSAGES
FLORIDA STATE SEMINOLE

2 (8-ounce) bottles chili sauce
2 (8-ounce) jars grape jelly
2 or 3 packages cocktail sausages

Mix all ingredients in a crock-pot or boiler for 2 hours or until mixture has permeated sausages. Serve warm. *This dish can be prepared the day before the game and refrigerated. Use sterno canned heat to serve warm.*

"FIRE UP TO WIN" SHRIMP
ALABAMA CRIMSON TIDE

1 pound medium shrimp in shells, uncooked
1/4 cup butter or margarine
1/4 cup vegetable oil
2 tablespoons lemon juice
1/4 teaspoon salt
1/4 teaspoon pepper
2 tablespoons barbecue sauce
1 bay leaf, crumbled
1 garlic clove, crushed
1/2 teaspoon dried basil leaves
1/2 teaspoon dried rosemary leaves
1/2 teaspoon paprika
1/2 teaspoon crushed dried red peppers

Butterfly shrimp by cutting lengthwise down back, not cutting all the way through. Do not remove shell. In a large skillet, melt butter or margarine. Add shrimp. Sauté 3 to 4 minutes until shrimp begins to turn pink. Add remaining ingredients. Simmer over low heat 3 to 4 minutes, stirring occasionally. Cover and let stand about 5 minutes. Spoon shrimp and sauce into a large serving bowl. Makes 35 to 40 servings.

CRAWFISH ETOUFFEE
LOUISIANA STATE TIGER

2 1/2 pounds crawfish tails
1 cup chopped onion
1/2 cup chopped celery
1/2 cup chopped bell pepper
1/3 cup green onion tops
3 cloves chopped garlic
1 stick margarine
2 tablespoons cornstarch
2 cups water
2 tablespoons Worcestershire sauce
5-6 cups cooked white rice

Sauté vegetables in pan with margarine on high heat. When onions begin to become opaque, reduce heat and add crawfish. Flavor with Worcestershire, salt, and pepper to your taste. Cook for 20-25 minutes. Add cornstarch and water. Stir well. Cook for additional 5-10 minutes. Serve over rice.

BAKED PARMESAN CHICKEN
GEORGIA BULLDOG

1 cup bread crumbs
1/3 cup grated Parmesan cheese
1/4 teaspoon ground oregano
1/4 teaspoon pepper
Salt, to taste
1 clove garlic, minced or garlic powder
3/4 cup melted butter or margarine, divided
1 (3-pound) chicken, cut up

Combine bread crumbs, cheese, oregano, pepper, and salt; set aside. Lightly sauté garlic in 2 tablespoons butter. Stir in remaining butter. Dip chicken in garlic butter. Roll each piece in bread crumb mixture. Place chicken in a 13 x 9 x 2-inch pan. Sprinkle with remaining bread crumb mixture and pour on remaining garlic butter. Bake at 350 degrees for 55 minutes or until golden brown. Serves 6.

BUFFALO WINGS
GEORGIA BULLDOG

1 package chicken wings
1/2 stick butter
1 bottle hot sauce
Cooking oil

Wash; then cut wings apart. Discard wing tips. Heat cooking oil. Fry wings until crispy. While wings are cooking, melt butter and add hot sauce. When wings are done, drain and add sauce mixture. Wings may be dipped in bleu cheese, if desired.

CHEESY CHICKEN
GEORGIA BULLDOG

6 chicken breast halves, cooked and boned
1 bunch fresh broccoli or 2 (10-ounce) packages frozen broccoli spears
1 (12 ounce) package of cream cheese
1 1/2 cup milk
1 teaspoon garlic salt
1/4 teaspoon salt
1/8 teaspoon white pepper
1 cup grated Parmesan cheese, divided
1/2 pound mushrooms, sautéed (optional)
1 (2.8-ounce) can onion rings

Cut chicken into large strips. Cook broccoli spears until tender. Melt cream cheese in milk over low heat. Add garlic salt, salt, pepper, and 3/4 cup Parmesan cheese to the cream cheese and milk mixture. Arrange broccoli on bottom of 2 quart rectangular baking dish. Layer mushrooms on top, if desired. Pour 1 cup of cheese mixture over broccoli. Lay chicken strips on top. Cover with remaining cheese mixture. Sprinkle with remaining 1 1/4 cups Parmesan cheese. Bake, covered, at 350 degrees for 15 minutes. Remove cover and bake an additional 15 minutes or until thoroughly heated. Sprinkle with onion rings during last 5 minutes of baking.

SPICY BEEF BRISKET AND SAUCE
AUBURN TIGER

3- to 4-pound well-trimmed brisket
1 teaspoon meat tenderizer
1/4 teaspoon seasoning salt
1/4 teaspoon celery seed
1/4 teaspoon garlic salt
3 tablespoons Liquid Smoke
1/4 cup Worcestershire sauce

Sprinkle both sides of meat with salts. Place in shallow container. Spoon Liquid Smoke and Worcestershire sauce on top. Cover and refrigerate 24 hours. Bake, uncovered, at 225 degrees for 3 to 4 hours. Chill; then slice thin and serve with sauce.

Sauce:
1/4 cup vinegar
1/2 lemon, thinly sliced
1/2 cup water
1/2 teaspoon pepper
2 tablespoons sugar
1/2 teaspoon salt
1 medium onion, grated
1 tablespoon prepared mustard
1/4 cup butter
1/4 teaspoon Tabasco sauce
2 tablespoons catsup

Combine first 9 ingredients in a saucepan, mixing well. Bring to a boil. Reduce heat and simmer 20 minutes. Stir in Tabasco sauce and catsup. Return to boil. Remove from heat and discard lemon. Serve meat and sauce on small buns or rolls.

SOWING WILD OATS

In the week prior to the 1947 LSU-Tulane game, Tiger faithful secretly planted oats in the playing field of Tulane Stadium. The oats sprang up, spelling out the letters "LSU."

LOUISIANA SPAGHETTI UNLIMITED
LOUISIANA STATE TIGER

1 stick oleo
1 onion, chopped
1 can Rotel Tomatoes
1 (16-ounce) package of Velveeta cheese
1 package spaghetti
4 chicken breasts

Melt oleo, onion, tomatoes, and cheese to gether. Boil chicken
breasts until tender. Debone, cut into pieces, and place in
casserole dish. Boil spaghetti in chicken broth until tender.
Drain and place in casserole. Top with cheese sauce. Bake 350
degrees for 30 minutes. Cover with foil and head for the
stadium parking lot!

CHICKEN BALLS FOR AUBURN OR CLEMSON
GEORGIA BULLDOG

2 cups ground or minced cooked chicken
1 can cream of mushroom soup
2 tablespoons mayonnaise
1 tablespoon minced onion
2 tablespoons lemon juice
1 cup soft bread crumbs
1 egg
Salt and pepper, to taste
Dry bread crumbs

Mix first 8 ingredients. Shape into balls or logs. Roll in the dry
bread crumbs and fry in vegetable oil until brown. Drain on paper towels.

DANCIN' WITH OLE MISS

Prior to many Ole Miss games in Oxford, fans gather at the
student union to toe-tap to a live Dixieland band, mingle, and
toss football footballs in a large shaded hardwood grove
nearby.
Even fans from visiting schools admit getting goose bumps

when the Rebel team and marching band walk through the grove en route to the stadium and the band strikes up Ole Miss' traditional fight songs.

CHICKEN FLORENTINE QUICHE
GEORGIA TECH YELLOW JACKET

9-inch unbaked prepared pie shell, thawed
1 (10-3/4-ounce) can chicken vegetable soup
3 eggs, slightly beaten
1 cup dry curd cottage cheese
1/2 cup grated Parmesan cheese
1/2 cup well drained cooked, chopped spinach
1/4 cup finely chopped onion
1/2 teaspoon oregano leaves, crushed

Prick pie shell with fork. Bake at 350 degrees for 10 minutes. Combine the remaining ingredients and pour into the pie shell. Bake at 350 degrees for 1 hour or until a knife, inserted in the center, comes out clean. Let stand 15 minutes before serving.

CURRY CHICKEN
SOUTH CAROLINA GAMECOCK

1 (8-ounce) package of cream cheese
1 cup chopped chicken
3/4 cup chopped almonds
1/3 cup mayonnaise
2 tablespoons chutney
1 tablespoon curry

Combine ingredients and shape into ball. Chill 2 hours. Cover with chopped parsley.

FOOTBALL CLASSICS

Football movies have always been popular, but some of the best films were made in the 1940s and '50s. Fred MacMurray played a troubled coach in the 1949 film *Father Was A Full-*

back. John Derek portrayed a college football player with lofty goals in the 1951 movie *Saturday's Hero.* Perhaps the most famous film of this era starred Ronald Reagan as Notre Dame player George Gipp in the 1940 classic *Knute Rockne—All American.*

EGG ROLL TIDES
ALABAMA CRIMSON TIDE

Coleslaw mix (pre-grated cabbage and carrots, found in grocery produce section)
Onion, chopped
Soy sauce
Cooked fresh or leftover chicken
Egg roll wrappers (in produce section)
Duck sauce

Stir-fry cabbage, carrots, and onion. Add meat and soy sauce until dry. May need to pat dry with a paper towel. Put mixture in egg roll. Roll up. Use a drop of water to seal. Drop in hot grease in Fry Daddy. Fry until golden. Let cool on paper towel. DO NOT STACK. Serve with duck sauce as dip.

THE CUB PRESIDENT

In 1935, Alabama was invited to play in the 1935 Rose Bowl in Pasadena. An unknown cub reporter was assigned to cover the Tide practice sessions in southern California. The rookie reporter, Ronald Reagan, was later elected President.

OLD COLLEGE CHEERS

Some of the original football rallying cries from the early 1900s were quite animated. Many sounded like a Dr. Suess rhyme. You would be hard pressed to hear them today.

At Alabama, fans hollered, "Rah, hoo, ree! Universitee! Rah, hoo! Wah, hoo! A.C.U." Notre Dame faithful once screamed, "Reh! reh! reh! U.D.U., N.D.U. reh! reh! reh!" In Nashville, you could have heard, "Vanderbilt, Rah, Rah, Rah! Whiz Boom! Zip-boom, Rah, Rah, Rah!" Fans really let loose at Illinois: "Rah-hoo-rah, Zip boom ah! Hip-zoo, Jimmy blow your baoo. Ip-sidi-iki, U. of I., Champaign?"

TIGER DELIGHT CHICKEN
AUBURN TIGER

1 cup mayonnaise
1/2 cup honey
2 tablespoons Chinese hot mustard
1 teaspoon sesame oil
1/2 teaspoon ground ginger
4 boneless, skinless chicken breast halves (about 1 1/4 pounds), cut into strips
2 cups finely crushed potato chips
2 tablespoons sesame seeds

Heat oven to 425 degrees. Mix honey, mayonnaise, mustard, oil, and ginger. Brush chicken with 1/2 cup of the mayonnaise mixture. Coat with combined crushed chips and sesame seeds. Place on greased cookie sheet. Bake 7-9 minutes. Turn; continue baking 4-5 minutes or until browned. Serve with remaining mayonnaise mixture as dipping sauce. Makes 8 appetizer servings.

HOMEMADE MACARONI AND CHEESE
MISSISSIPPI STATE BULLDOG

1 pound elbow macaroni
1 poundVelveeta cheese
1 small onion, minced
1/2 cup milk
Margarine

Cook the macaroni according to package directions. Drain. Butter a 2-quart casserole. Layer the bottom with minced onion. Add a layer of macaroni, then a layer of Velveeta sliced in 1/4 inch sections. Repeat the macaroni and cheese layers until the dish is full. Pour the milk evenly over the casserole. Bake in a 350 degree oven until brown and bubbly. Keep cool until served. Better served warm but still good cold, straight out of the ice chest.

GREEN BEAN CASSEROLE
GEORGIA TECH YELLOW JACKET

2 medium onions, sliced
3 packages frozen French beans
1 package slivered almonds
1 pint sour cream
1 stick butter or margarine
1/2 cup grated sharp cheese

Sauté onions and almonds in butter. Cook beans about 5 minutes. Drain. Mix all ingredients with sour cream. Cook at 350 degrees until bubbly.

VARSITY VEG-ALL
LOUISIANA STATE TIGERS

2 (16-ounce) cans Veg-All vegetables
1/2 cup chopped onions
1 (8 1/2) ounce drained can water chestnuts
1 cup sharp grated cheese
3/4 cup mayonnaise
2 cups crushed Ritz crackers

Mix first 5 ingredients and top with crackers. Bake 30 minutes in lightly-greased casserole dish at 350 degrees.

EARTH QUAKERS

A strange thing happened in Baton Rouge, Louisiana, on October 8, 1988—an event LSU fans call "The Night the Tigers Moved the Earth."

With 1:41 left to play in a tight game against Auburn, LSU's Tommy Hodgson hit Eddie Fulmer with a touchdown pass to tie the game. It was 9:32 p.m., and the partisan crowd of 79,431 jumped and screamed so loudly that a tremor caused by the stadium vibrations registered as a large block of ink on a seismograph in LSU's Geology Department on campus. LSU kicked the extra point and won the game, 7-6.

CHEESE GRITS
GEORGIA BULLDOG

1 cup grits
4 cups water
1/2 pound sharp cheese, grated
1/2 stick butter or margarine
4 eggs
1 teaspoon salt

Cook grits according to package; then stir in cheese. Add butter and then the eggs, 1 at a time. Beat well. Pour into buttered casserole. Bake at 375 degrees for 45 minutes, uncovered. For best results, let stand 5 to 10 minutes before serving to allow the grits to become firm. Serves a lot. *This can be warmed over successfully. This is also a great dish for a covered dish banquet or fancy breakfast. You won't regret trying this one!*

TAR HEELS

Athletic teams at the University of North Carolina are called Tar Heels because North Carolina is known as the Tar Heel State. Two different stories exist about the origin of the nickname. A key element in both stories is the fact that the production of tar, pitch, and turpentine was for many years the state's principal industry.

One account goes back to the Revolutionary War. According to this story, troops of British General Cornwallis were crossing what is now known as the Tar River between Rocky Mount and Battleboro when they discovered that tar had been dumped into the stream to impede their crossing. When they finally got across the river, they found their feet completely black with tar. Their observation that anyone who waded North Carolina rivers would get tar heels led to the nickname.

The other popular theory can be traced back to the Civil War. During one of the war's fiercest battles, a column supporting North Carolina troops was driven from the field. After the battle, the North Carolinians who had successfully fought it out alone, met the regiment which had fled to safety and were greeted with the question, "Any more tar down in the Old North State, boys?"

"No, not a bit," shot back one of the North Carolina soldiers. "Old Jeff's bought it all up," he said, referring to Confederate President Jefferson Davis.

"Is that so? What's he going to do with it?"

"He's going to put it on you'ns heels to make you stick better in the next fight."

Upon hearing of the incident, Robert E. Lee smiled and said to a fellow officer, "God bless the Tar Heel boys."

STRESS RELIEF

Football coaches feel great pressure to win games. When they don't, humor can be a great stress reliever.

When Mack Brown coached at Tulane, his Green Wave team opened one season with seven straight losses. Seeking Divine Intervention, Brown said, he called Dial-a-Prayer "and they hung up on me."

When Ken Hatfield was head coach at Arkansas, someone asked Razorback athletic director Frank Broyles if he'd still like Hatfield if his team won only half its games. "Sure I would," Broyles said. "I'd miss him, too."

Former Texas coach Darrell Royal said that every head coach's first objective is to coax fanatical efforts from his players.

"He wants his team to play on Saturday as if they were planting the flag on Iwo Jima," he said.

🍴

Fourth Quarter Stand

7

Cookies
and
Desserts

NOTES

7

Cookies and Desserts

Offering a variety of edibles enhances any tailgate picnic. We've never seen a pregame party without some type of sweet snack on the table. Some people arrive late and may pass on the heavier dishes. But where there are desserts, there are people.

CARAMEL COOKIES
GEORGIA BULLDOG

1/2 cup melted margarine
1/2 cup melted butter
1 cup firmly packed brown sugar
1 cup chopped pecans
18 (5-inch-long) graham crackers, halved

Combine margarine, butter, sugar, and pecans in a saucepan. Bring to a rolling boil over low heat; boil 3 minutes, stirring constantly. Place graham crackers in a 15 x 10 x1 pan; spoon butter mixture over crackers. Bake at 350 for 10 to 12 minutes. Cut into squares. Makes 36 cookies.

THE EGG BOWL

Ecstatic Ole Miss fans were beaten back with cane bottom chairs while trying to tear down the goal posts after upsetting rival Mississippi A&M College in 1926. Newspapers called it "The Battle of Starkville."

To ease tensions, both schools in 1927 agreed to share the cost of creating "The Golden Egg," a gold-plated football mounted on a pedestal. The winner each year takes home the coveted trophy, and the game's score is engraved on the pedestal.

In years when the teams tie, the previous year's winner keeps the trophy half the year, and then it's passed to the other school. Since 1978, the Mississippi media have called the annual Ole Miss-Mississippi State clash "The Egg Bowl."

NO BAKE OATMEAL COOKIES
FLORIDA GATOR

3 cups oatmeal
1/2 cup milk
1 cup pecans
2 cups sugar
1/4 cup cocoa
3 tablespoons peanut butter

Mix cocoa, milk, sugar, and peanut butter in a heavy saucepan. Boil only 2 minutes after it reaches a rolling boil. Pour over oatmeal and nuts. Drop onto waxed paper.

NUTTY NO BAKE COOKIES
GEORGIA BULLDOG

2 cups sugar
1/2 cup peanut butter
1/4 cup margarine
2 cups chopped nuts
1/2 cup milk
1 teaspoon vanilla
4 tablespoons cocoa

Combine sugar, butter, cocoa, and milk. Boil 1 minute. Stir in nuts, peanut butter, and vanilla. Drop from spoon on waxed paper.

GATOR CREATORS

How did the Florida Gators get that nickname? In 1907, Austin Miller, a native of Gainesville, was enrolled in the University of Virginia. His father, Phillip Miller, a Gainesville merchant, came to visit him. While in Charlottesville, Mr. Miller decided to order some pennants and banners for the University of Florida from the Michie Company. The Millers went to the firm, where they were shown pennants of other colleges. When the manager asked for Florida's nickname and emblem, both father and son realized that Florida had none; Austin then suggested the name Alligators because the alligator was native to Florida. Unfortunately, the Michie manager had never seen an alligator; therefore, he couldn't design one. After Austin located a picture in the University of Virginia library, the Michie firm designed an emblem. In 1908, Philip Miller's store carried the blue banners measuring six by three feet, showing a large orange alligator. The pennants proved to be popular with Florida students, and the nickname was launched.

SIX-LAYER HOG TREAT
ARKANSAS RAZORBACK

1 stick margarine
1 cup crushed graham crackers
1 cup chocolate chips
1 cup butterscotch chips
1 cup pecans
1 cup coconut, shredded or flaked
1 can Eagle Brand condensed milk

Melt margarine in an 8x11 pan. Spread crushed graham crackers over margarine. Layer chocolate chips, butterscotch chips, pecans, and coconut over crumbs. Pour Eagle Brand milk over all. Bake at 350 degrees for 30 minutes. Cool. Cut into squares and refrigerate.

SOUTH'S OLDEST

The first football game played in the Deep South was played at Piedmont Park in Atlanta on February 20, 1892. Auburn beat Georgia 10-0, to begin the South's longest continuous football rivalry and the nation's eighth oldest rivalry.

THE ULTIMATE BULLDOG CHOCOLATE CHIP COOKIE
GEORGIA BULLDOG

3/4 cup butter flavor Crisco
1 3/4 cup all purpose flour
1 1/4 cup packed brown sugar
1 teaspoon salt
2 tablespoons milk

3/4 teaspoon baking soda
1 tablespoon vanilla
1 cup semi-sweet chocolate chips
1 egg
1 cup pecan pieces (optional)

Heat oven to 375 degrees. Mix Crisco, brown sugar, milk, and vanilla. Blend until creamy. Blend in egg. Combine flour, salt, and baking soda. Gradually add to creamed mixture. Stir in chocolate chips and nuts. Drop rounded tablespoon of dough 3 inches apart on ungreased cookie sheet. Bake at 375 degrees for 8 to 10 minutes for chewy cookies. Cool on baking sheet for 2 minutes. *If nuts are omitted, add 1 1/2 cups semi-sweet chocolate chips.*

GEORGIA SOUTHERN FOOTBALL FACTS

World War II had a dramatic effect on Georgia Southern's athletic teams. When the U.S. declared war on Japan after the December 7, 1941, Pearl Harbor attack, the majority of the 1941 Blue Tide football team joined the war effort. After World War II, when all sports except football were revived, the nickname was changed to Professors to complement the name of the school then, Georgia Teachers College. When the school was renamed Georgia Southern College in 1959, Professors was dropped. The student body voted for a new name, and Eagles was selected in a narrow vote over Colonels.

After World War II ended in 1945, basketball and baseball returned to Georgia Southern University, but not football. The school had no team until 1981. Erk Russell, longtime Georgia defensive coordinator, shocked many people when he accepted the head coaching position. Since then, Georgia Southern has not had a losing season. Since joining the NCAA Division I-AA in 1984, GSU has won more games and a higher percentage of its games than any other I-AA team. The school won the national championship in 1985, 1986, 1989, and 1990.

The 1989 football squad became the first team this century to finish with a 15-0 mark.

Coach Erk Russell led the school to three of its four national championships before he retired from coaching in December 1989. Inducted into the Georgia Sports Hall of Fame in

1987, he received numerous awards including the Eddie Robinson Award (for top Division I-AA coach) in 1989.

GRANDMOTHER'S COOKIES
SOUTHERN MISSISSIPPI GOLDEN EAGLE

1/2 cup oleo
3/4 cup sugar
1 egg
1 teaspoon vanilla extract
1/2 teaspoon almond extract
1 tablespoon milk
1 1/4 cups flour
1/2 teaspoon salt
1/2 teaspoon baking powder

Cream oleo and sugar. Add milk, egg, vanilla, and almond. Sift flour; mix other dry ingredients together & add to flour. Bake 8 minutes at 375 degrees.

Variations:

1. Add 1/2 cup coconut.
2. Omit vanilla; add 2 tablespoons lemon rind and 1 teaspoon lemon juice.
3. Add 1/2 cup pecans.
4. Use orange juice for milk; add 2 tablespoons rind and 1 extra egg yolk.
5. Add 1/3 cup dry cocoa or 2 ounces unsweetened melted chocolate. Bake 325 degrees.

Any variation makes about 3-4 dozen cookies.

THE GEORGIA WAREAGLE

Pepper WarEagle White grew up in an Auburn family. Her parents, who met as Auburn students, have taken Pepper and her sister, Whitney Tiger White, to Auburn games since the girls were babies. They even named their daughters after Auburn's famous mascot and battle cry.

Pepper shocked her Vestavia Hills, Alabama, friends when she announced plans to enroll at the University of Georgia in the fall of 1994—an Alabamian named WarEagle in the heart of Bulldog country. But her parents took it well.

"We want her to love Georgia as much as we love Auburn," said her mom, Kaye White.

BIG AL COCOA PEANUT LOGS
ALABAMA CRIMSON TIDE

1 cup (6 ounces) semi-sweet chocolate pieces
1/3 cup peanut butter
4 cups Kellogg's cocoa Krispies

Melt chocolate pieces with peanut butter over hot, but not boiling, water. Stir until well blended. Remove from heat. Add cocoa Krispies. Stir until completely coated with chocolate mixture. Press into lightly buttered 9 x 9 pan. Let stand until hardened. Cut into 36 log-shaped bars, about 3/4 x 3 inches.

EVERY BULLDOG'S FAVORITE CHOCOLATE CHIP COOKIE
MISSISSIPPI STATE BULLDOG

1 cup plus 2 tablespoons all-purpose flour
1/2 teaspoon baking soda
1/2 teaspoon salt
1/2 cup butter, softened
1/2 cup (packed) brown sugar
1/3 cup granulated sugar
1/2 teaspoon vanilla
1 egg
1 (6-ounce) package semi-sweet chocolate chips

Combine flour, soda, and salt; set aside. Beat butter, both sugars, and vanilla in large bowl. Beat in egg. Slowly add flour mixture, stirring well. Stir in chips. Drop by teaspoon onto ungreased baking sheet. Bake at 375 degrees for 9-11 minutes. Makes about 2 dozen cookies.

SWIRL BROWNIES
FLORIDA STATE SEMINOLE

1 (20- to 23-ounce) package brownie mix
1 (8-ounce) package cream cheese, softened
1/3 cup sugar
1 egg
1/2 teaspoon vanilla

Prepare brownie mix as directed on package. Combine cream cheese and sugar, mixing until well blended. Blend in egg and vanilla. Reserve 1/2 cup batter. Spread remaining batter onto bottom of greased 13 x 9 baking pan. Cover with cream cheese mixture. Spoon on reserved batter. Cut through batter with knife several times for marble effect. Bake at 350 degrees for 35 to 40 minutes or until cream cheese mixture is lightly browned. Cool for 2 hours. Cut into squares. Makes 1 1/2 dozen.

LSU FOOTBALL FACTS

LSU was the first college team to ever play on foreign soil. On Christmas Day in 1907, the football team traveled to Cuba where they stomped the University of Havana team, 56-0.

The Tigers won the national football championship in 1958 with an 11-0 season. Halfback Billy Cannon won the Heisman Trophy that year. Cannon's performance against Ole Miss on Halloween night in 1959 is probably the most famous play in Tiger gridiron records, and some say, cinched the Heisman Trophy for him. That night, the Rebels took a 3-0 lead into the final quarter, threatening to end an 18-game LSU winning streak, when Cannon made a 89-yard punt return to win the game.

THE MAN IN STRIPES

Clemson University's well-known mascot is the costumed one known simply as The Tiger, sometimes called the man in stripes. The mascot was first instituted 37 years ago. Today, students go through extensive try-outs and auditions to win the coveted job. The biggest Tiger tradition of all is the pushup tradition, which began in 1978 when mascot Zack Mills began doing pushups for every point Clemson scored.

MSU MINT BROWNIES
MISSISSIPPI STATE BULLDOG

Brownies

4 large eggs
2 cups sugar
1 cup all-purpose flour
1 cup cocoa
1 cup butter or margarine, melted
1 teaspoon vanilla extract
1/2 teaspoon peppermint extract

Beat eggs lightly with wisk in large mixing bowl. Add sugar and stir well. Combine flour and cocoa; gradually stir into egg mixture. Stir in melted butter and flavorings. Pour into greased 15 x 10 x 1 inch jellyroll pan; bake at 350 degrees for 15 to 18 minutes or until toothpick comes out clean. Cool in pan on wire rack.

Mint Cream Frosting

1/4 cup butter, softened
1 3/4 cups sifted powered sugar
1 to 3 tablespoons milk
1/2 teaspoon peppermint extract
3 to 4 drops green food coloring

Beat butter at medium speed with an electric mixer; gradually add sugar, beating after each addition. Add milk; beat until spreading consistency. Stir in peppermint extract and food coloring. Spread the Mint Frosting over cooled brownie layer; freeze for 15 minutes.

Chocolate Frosting

3 (1-ounce) squares unsweetened chocolate
3 tablespoons butter or margarine

Melt chocolate squares and 3 tablespoons of butter in microwave. Spread over mint frosted brownies with pastry brush. Refrigerate until firm. Cut and store in refrigerator or ice chest. *A hit at any tailgate party!*

Herschel Walker awed all who witnessed his power and speed for the first time, especially during the Heisman Trophy winner's freshman season at Georgia in 1980.

He simply ran past, or over, defenders who stepped in his way.

Walker's running style prompted a songwriter to remark that "Herschel didn't know where he was going, but he was going somewhere in a hurry!"

Herschel, known to play while injured, said "pain is sometimes in your head."

CHEESECAKE BARS
GEORGIA BULLDOG

5 tablespoons butter
1/3 cup brown sugar
1 cup flour
3/4 cup chopped nuts
1/2 cup sugar
1 (8-ounce) package cream cheese
1 egg
2 tablespoons milk
1 tablespoon lemon juice
1/4 teaspoon vanilla extract

Cream butter and brown sugar. Add flour and nuts and mix. Set aside 1 cup mixture for topping. Press remainder in bottom of 8 x 8 baking pan. Bake at 350 degrees for 12 to 15 minutes. Blend sugar and cream cheese until smooth. Add egg, milk, lemon juice, and vanilla. Beat well. Spread over bottom crust. Sprinkle with reserved 1 cup of topping. Return to oven and bake for 25 minutes more. Cool. Cut into squares.

JOB SECURITY

Prior to the 1945 season, 22 different coaches took a turn as head coach at Ole Miss. Only seven of those coaches lasted for more than one season.

John Vaught, who was Ole Miss' winningest coach, won 185 games and three national titles between 1946 and 1970, when failing health forced his retirement.

Vaught was replaced by Billy Kinard, the first Ole Miss alumnus to serve as head football coach. Only three games into the 1973 season, Kinard and Ole Miss athletic director Frank "Bruiser" Kinard were fired following two straight non-SEC losses and reports of team dissension.

Vaught, then 64, came out of retirement to fill both positions, and won five of the next eight games. He retired as head coach at the end of the 1973 season, but remained as athletic director.

CHESS SQUARES
SOUTHERN MISSISSIPPI GOLDEN EAGLE

1 pound box brown sugar
1 cup white sugar
2 sticks oleo
4 eggs
1 teaspoon vanilla extract
2 cups sifted flour
1 teaspoon baking powder
1/2 teaspoon salt
1 cup pecans

Separate eggs. Beat egg whites until stiff, but not dry. Melt oleo and add to sugars in mixing bowl. Beat until smooth. Add flour, baking powder, and salt to cream sugar/butter mixture; then add vanilla and pecans. Fold in egg whites. Pour in 13 x 9 inch pan. Bake 350 degrees 25-30 minutes. Cool in pan before cutting.

LAYDOWN BOYS

The final game of the 1971 regular season found Florida at the Orange Bowl to play host Miami. Gator quarterback John Reaves needed 344 passing yards going into the game to break the collegiate passing yards total held by Jim Plunkett. With Florida leading 45-8 with about 90 seconds to play and Miami deep in Gator territory, Florida Coach Doug Dickey made a controversial decision.

Dickey okayed his defense to fall to the ground on Miami's next snap—allowing the Hurricanes to easily score and return the ball to Florida. The reason: give Reaves, who then only needed 14 yards, a final chance to break the record.

Two snaps later, Reaves connected with Carlos Alvarez for 15 yards and the NCAA record.

ROLL TIDE GINGERBREAD
ALABAMA CRIMSON TIDE

1 1/2 cups sifted flour
1 teaspoon baking soda
1 teaspoon ginger
1/8 teaspoon salt
1/3 cup shortening
1/2 cup sugar
1 egg
1/2 cup molasses
3/4 cup boiling water
Applesauce (optional)

Sift together flour, baking soda, ginger, and salt. Set aside. Using electric mixer, cream shortening until light and fluffy. Add sugar gradually. Beat in egg. Blend in molasses. Gradually stir dry ingredients into creamed mixture. Beat thoroughly. Stir in water. Turn into greased and floured 8" square pan. Bake at 350 for 40 minutes. Top with applesauce if desired. *Enjoy on a crisp autumn afternoon.*

BULLDOG PEANUT BUTTER CHOCOLATE SWIRL FUDGE
GEORGIA BULLDOG

1/2 cup light or dark corn syrup
1/3 cup evaporated milk
3 cups semi-sweet chocolate morsels
2 teaspoons vanilla
3/4 cup powdered sugar, sifted
1/3 cup extra crunchy peanut butter

Grease an 8-inch baking pan. In a heavy 2-quart saucepan, stir together corn syrup and milk. Add chocolate morsels. Stirring constantly, cook over medium-low heat until chocolate is melted. Remove from heat. Stir in vanilla. Add powdered sugar. Beat until smooth. Turn into pan. Spoon peanut butter over fudge into small dollops. With small spatula, swirl fudge to marbleize. Refrigerate 2 hours or until firm. Cut into squares. Makes 1 1/2 pounds.

INCREDIBLE TIDE EDIBLES
ALABAMA CRIMSON TIDE

1 cup graham cracker crumbs
2 cups powdered sugar
3/4 cup melted margarine
1 (12-ounce) jar crunchy peanut butter
1 (12-ounce) package semi-sweet chocolate pieces

Combine graham cracker crumbs, sugar, margarine, and peanut butter. Put in greased 13 x 9 x 2 inch baking pan. Melt chocolate pieces. Spread over cookie mix. Refrigerate until set. Cut into squares. Store in tightly covered container. Yields 3 dozen. YUMMY!

THE LONELY END

Army debuted a new offensive strategy on Sept. 27, 1958, against South Carolina—a tactic that helped the Cadets to an 8-win season.

On the game's first play, the Army offense huddled for the play call—all, that is, except number 87, Bill Carpenter. The Cadet end stood alone 15 yards from the huddle, hands on hips, and watched the quarterback, Joe Caldwell. Carpenter ran his route perfectly.

Carpenter's ability to complete his assignments without huddling upset the Gamecocks' defense and proved to be a psychological advantage. "The Lonely End," as the press dubbed Carpenter, received signals from the quarterback's feet movements.

PRALINES
GEORGIA BULLDOG

3 1/2 cups sugar
1 cup milk
1 stick margarine
3 cups pecans (not chopped)

In a small skillet or saucepan, brown 1/2 cup of sugar. In a large saucepan, place 3 cups sugar and 1 cup milk. Mix thoroughly and heat to boiling. When this mixture begins to boil and the 1/2 cup of sugar is completely brown and melted, remove both pans from heat. Pour the melted sugar into the large saucepan while stirring together. (It will bubble up, so be sure it is off the heat). When mixed thoroughly, replace on heat and bring to boil. Begin timing when it begins to boil and cook 9 minutes over medium heat. After 9 minutes, remove from heat; add margarine and let cool for about 5 minutes. Beat by hand until it begins to thicken (when sugar leaves a definite trail on the bottom of the pan). Add pecans and stir. Drop by spoonfuls onto foil, stirring and dipping from bottom while dropping in order to keep nuts distributed. Let cool. When candy is hardened, foil peels off easily.

PEACH CANDY
GEORGIA SOUTHERN EAGLE

1 pound dried peaches
2 cups 10X powdered sugar
1/2 cup orange juice
1 1/2 cups pecan halves

Chop up peaches in food processor or blender until finely ground. Add sugar and orange juice. Let stand for 10 minutes. Cook over low heat, stirring constantly for 10 minutes. Remove from heat and cool slightly. Add enough additional powdered sugar to make a stiff mixture. Take about 1 teaspoonful and wrap around each pecan half. Roll lightly in more powdered sugar and let stand in refrigerator overnight.

CHOCOLATE POUND CAKE FROSTING
OR "WONDERFUL FUDGE"
GEORGIA BULLDOG

2 cups sugar
1/4 cup cocoa
2/3 cup milk
1/2 cup melted Crisco shortening
2 teaspoons vanilla
Dash of salt

Combine sugar and cocoa. Add melted shortening and milk. Boil for 2 minutes, stirring constantly. Remove and add vanilla. Beat until creamy. Use for cake or add pecans to make fudge.

MARZIPANS
GEORGIA SOUTHERN EAGLE

1 can Solo almond paste
1 package puff pastry (Pepperidge Farm)
1 small jar apricot jam
1 1/3 sticks butter or margarine, melted
1 cup flour, sifted
3/4 cup sugar
2 eggs

About 10 minutes before preparing batter, carefully open up both Pepperidge Farm pastry sheets flat on counter and smooth back seams. When thawed, divide and cut each sheet into 12 sections. Butter muffin tins. Place 1 section of pastry into each section of tin and push into place. Prick bottom with a fork 1 time. Put about 1/2 teaspoon of jam into each section.

BATTER:

Combine all remaining ingredients except flour and beat with a hand mixer on fast for 3 minutes. Add flour slowly until thoroughly blended. Scoop generous amounts of batter on top of jam filled pastry sections. Bake both tins at 400 degrees for 20 minutes. *These Marzipans will melt in your mouth!*

MINCEMEAT SQUARES
GEORGIA BULLDOG

1 stick butter
1 1/4 cups quick oats
1 1/4 cups flour
1 jar mincemeat
1/2 teaspoon salt
1 cup cooked or canned apples
1 cup brown sugar
1 teaspoon soda
1/4 cup nuts

Mix together (until crumbly): butter, flour, soda, salt, and brown sugar. Add the quick oats. Put half of this mixture in 8 x 12 pan. Spread over this mincemeat, cooked apples, and nuts. Put remainder of the first mixture on top. Pack down and bake 45 minutes at 350 degrees. Cut in squares and let cool.

JENNY'S TIGER TURTLE BROWNIES
AUBURN TIGER

1 package German Chocolate cake mix
1 package caramels
1 (6-ounce) package chocolate chips
1 can evaporated milk
1 1/2 sticks margarine
1 cup chopped pecans or walnut
1 cup grated coconut
1 egg, slightly beaten

Heat oven to 350 degrees. Mix caramels, 1/2 cup milk, and 1/2 cup margarine on stove, stirring until melted or microwave 2 minutes, stir, then 1 or 2 minutes more. Set aside. Mix cake mix, rest of milk and margarine, egg, and pecans. Stir by hand until mixed well. In greased 9 x 12 pan, pour half of cake mix. Bake 10 minutes; remove from oven. Sprinkle chocolate chips, then coconut, then drizzle caramel over cake. Drop remaining cake mix by teaspoon over caramel. Bake about 20 minutes until cake is dry to touch. Cool completely and refrigerate until firm. Then cut into squares.

MINI CHEESECAKES
GEORGIA BULLDOG
AND GEORGIA TECH YELLOW JACKET

12 vanilla wafers
2 (8-ounce) packages cream cheese, softened
1/2 cup sugar
1 teaspoon vanilla
2 eggs

Line muffin tin with foil liners. Place 1 vanilla wafer in each liner. Mix cream cheese, vanilla, and sugar on medium speed until well blended. Add eggs. Mix well. Pour over wafers, filling 3/4 full. Bake for 25 minutes at 325 degrees. Remove from pan when cool. Top with fruit, preserves, nuts, or chocolate. Makes 12.

"Be as creative as you like when topping the cheesecakes," says Claire Sale Steagall, who offers this treat. Claire, a native Atlantan, was born into a family of die-hard Yellow Jackets, but was educated at Georgia. She can switch her loyalties to suit the occasion.

OOEGG
GEORGIA BULLDOG

1 box yellow cake mix
1 stick margarine
1 egg
1 cup nuts

Mix and put on bottom of a 9 x 13-inch pan. Do NOT melt butter; chop up.

8-ounce cream cheese
2 eggs
1 box confectioner's sugar

Mix and put on top of bottom mixture. Bake at 350 degrees for 40 minutes. Let cool.

APPLE CAKE
MISSISSIPPI STATE BULLDOG

4 cups chopped apples
1 teaspoon cinnamon
2 cups sugar
2 eggs
2 cups plain flour
2/3 cup oil
1 1/2 teaspoon soda
1 teaspoon vanilla
1 teaspoon salt
1 cup chopped pecans

Sift dry ingredients into apple mixture. Blend eggs and oil together. Combine all ingredients. Bake at 350 degrees for 40 to 50 minutes.

Glaze for Apple Cake:
1/2 cup light brown sugar
1/3 cup warm milk
1/2 cup margarine
1 teaspoon vanilla

Mix and pour Glaze over cake while still warm.

APPLE DELIGHT
TENNESSEE VOLUNTEER

1 cup brown sugar
2 cans apple pie filling
1 1/2 sticks margarine
1/2 cup chopped pecans
1 box yellow cake mix

Grease a 9 x 13 baking dish. Sprinkle sugar over the bottom of pan. Add pie filling, spreading evenly. Put cake mix on top of pie filling, covering evenly. Sprinkle pecans over mixture. Press down. Melt margarine and pour over the cake mix. Bake at 350 degrees for about 30 minutes. Serve with whipped cream or Cool Whip.

AUBURN ORANGE MINI CAKES
GEORGIA BULLDOG

1 box yellow cake mix

Prepare cake mix following directions on box. Use mini-muffin pan with liners. Bake in oven at temperature on box for 5 to 10 minutes. Dip immediately in Glaze (while hot). Dry on wax paper or on rack above paper.

GLAZE:
Peel of 1 lemon, ground
Juice of 2 oranges
Peel of 1 orange, ground
1 1/2 pounds confectioner's sugar
Juice of 2 lemons

Combine all ingredients. Mix well.

ICEBOX FRUITCAKE
AUBURN TIGER

1 box vanilla wafers
1 pound hulled nuts
1 pound mixed fruit
1 box white raisins
1 can coconut
1 can sweetened condensed milk
2 tablespoons water

Crush vanilla wafers. Mix in dry ingredients. Add milk and water and mix. Place in pyrex pan or fruit cake tin. Store in refrigerator for 3 or 4 days.

HEISMAN'S SHADOW

Auburn is the only university where John Heisman coached to have a Heisman Trophy winner. Tiger winners were Pat Sullivan in 1971 and Bo Jackson in 1985.

QUICK TRIFLE
GEORGIA TECH YELLOW JACKET

1 large package instant vanilla pudding
Angel Food cake or pound cake, broken into pieces

Layer the cake and pudding, making 2 layers each.

PINEAPPLE POUND CAKE
GEORGIA SOUTHERN EAGLE

3 cups sugar
2 cups vegetable shortening
10 eggs
3 cups all purpose flour
1 pinch salt
1 small can crushed pineapple, drained (reserve the juice)

Cream sugar and shortening thoroughly. Add flour one cup at a
time with 4 eggs, alternately adding 3 eggs each additional
time. Add salt. Stir in pineapple. Pour into greased and floured
tube pan. Bake at 300 degrees for 1 1/2 hours.

Optional Glaze:
1/2 cup sugar
1 tablespoon margarine
Reserved pineapple juice

Cook until thick when dropped from spoon. Spread over warm,
unmolded cake.

APPLE CRUMB PIE
GEORGIA BULLDOG

Filling:
6 Granny Smith apples
1 teaspoon ground cinnamon
1/2 cup brown sugar
1 teaspoon vanilla
1/4 cup flour

2 tablespoons lemon juice
1 teaspoon ground nutmeg
1 1/2 tablespoons margarine

Preheat oven to 350 degrees. Peel, slice apples. Melt butter. Mix all ingredients together. Stir into unbaked pie shell.

Topping:
1 cup flour
1/2 cup brown sugar
1/2 cup butter or margarine

Melt butter. Mix flour, butter, and brown sugar. Mixture will be crumbly. Spread over apple filling. Bake at 350 degrees until apples are tender and top is light brown. *This pie is great served warm with ice cream..*

BLUEBERRY CREAM PIE
FLORIDA STATE SEMINOLE

1 box Dream Whip (prepare according to package directions)
3 cups sifted 4X powdered sugar
1 (8-ounce) package cream cheese, softened
1 can blueberry pie filling
1 cup pecans

Mix cream cheese and sugar and fold in Dream Whip. Press pecans into pastry shells before baking. Put cream cheese mixture into baked pie shells and top with 1 can of blueberry pie filling (Comstock brand). This recipe should be divided into 2 pies.

OPTIONAL CRUST:
Cut 2 sticks of butter or margarine into 2 cups self-rising flour and press 1 cup chopped nuts into mixture after pressing into Pyrex dish. Bake at 350 degrees until brown.

GOOD BUY

George Woodruff, a wealthy businessman from Columbus, Georgia, coached the Georgia Bulldogs from 1923 through 1927 for only $1 per year.

CLAUDETTE'S "DAWG RICH" PIE
MISSISSIPPI STATE BULLDOG

Large container Cool Whip
1 small can condensed lemonade
1 (8-ounce) cream cheese
1 can Eagle Brand condensed milk
1 can pineapple tidbits
1/2 cup coconut
1 can cherry pie filling

Mix Cool Whip, lemonade, cream cheese, and condensed milk with mixer. Add pineapple tidbits and coconut. Mix. Pour into 2 graham cracker crusts. Pour cherry pie filling on top. Chill. Tastes best if refrigerated overnight.

CHOCOLATE BAR PIE
SOUTH CAROLINA GAMECOCK

1 chocolate pie shell
1 (6-count) package Hershey's plain candy bar
1 (12-ounce) container of Cool Whip

Melt Hershey's bars in a microwave on low or in a saucepan on the stove until liquid. Add to Cool Whip. Mix with hand mixer until creamy. Pour into pie shell. Chill in freezer until firm. Serve.

PECAN ICE CREAM SUNDAE SAUCE
LOUISIANA STATE TIGER

2 cups pecan halves, dry roasted
1 cup light corn syrup
1 cup dark corn syrup
1/2 pound (2 sticks) unsalted butter
1/4 teaspoon butterscotch flavoring

In a large skillet, combine pecan halves and corn syrups. Over high heat, stir constantly until mixture reaches a boil. Remove from heat. Add butter and stir until melted; then stir in butterscotch flavoring. For each serving, spoon some of the pecans and about 1/4 cup syrup (warm or at outdoor temperature) over 2 scoops of ice cream, which can be stored in bottom of ice-filled cooler until ready to serve. *DO NOT REFRIGERATE.*

RAMNAPPING

A white ram named Rameses is the North Carolina Tar Heel mascot. In 1924, cheerleader Vic Huggins thought of a ram as a mascot by linking it with the nickname of Tar Heel star Jack Merritt, a fullback known as "The Battering Ram." In 1922, Merritt had acquired the nickname for the way he plunged into lines.

Prior to the Duke game, Rameses tries to outwit Blue Devil students trying to ramnap him. An old story that Richard Nixon, while a law student at Duke, was involved in an attempt to heist Rameses was denied by the White House during his presidency.

YELLOW JACKETS

Georgia Tech's famous nickname and mascot did not originate from the familiar flying insect. The insect mascot, instead, grew out of the name "yellow jackets."

Historians say the first reference to Tech students as "Yellow Jackets" appeared in 1905 in the *Atlanta Constitution.* The name, at first spelled as one word, first described Tech supporters who arrived at games in Atlanta dressed in yellow coats and jackets. Tech's school colors are white and gold.

The engineering school's famous Rambling Wreck car, a pre-1940s roadster that leads the Tech football team onto the Grant Field at Bobby Dodd Stadium, was discovered while parked in front of a university vice-president's apartment building.

MIKE THE TIGER

Before a live tiger became a tradition for LSU athletic teams, a very realistic papier-mache tiger was used for more than a decade. Then in 1935, Mike the Tiger was purchased from the Little Rock Zoo by the student body for $750. Originally known as Sheik, his name was changed to Mike in honor of Mike Chambers, who served as LSU's athletic trainer when the mascot was purchased. Mike I reigned for 20 years before dying of pneumonia. Mike II served only one season, also dying of pneumonia. Mike III, purchased from the Seattle Zoo by the student body for $1,500, served 18 years as mascot. Mike IV, who hailed from Florida, served 14 years. A tiger from Alabama, Mike V began his reign on April 30, 1990, when he moved into the tiger cage across from Tiger Stadium.

Tradition says that for every growl by Mike the Tiger before a football game, the Tigers will score a touchdown that night.

NO U TURNS

Every football player makes mistakes, but most are quickly forgotten. California lineman Roy Riegel's error in the 1929 Rose Bowl against Georgia Tech is legendary.

Riegel, a center, scooped up a Tech fumble, crossed the field, and turned the corner to race for a touchdown. More than 66,000 fans were shocked as Riegel streaked 80 yards the *wrong way* toward his own goal line. Riegel made it to the end zone, but a teammate who had been in desperate pursuit yanked him back to the one-yard-line before Tech's pursuers tackled him.

On the next play, California tried to punt out of danger, but Tech blocked it and scored a two-point safety. Georgia Tech won the game, 8-7.

🍴

Victory Party

8

Tips for a Winning Tailgate

NOTES

❦ 8 ❦

Tips for a Winning Tailgate

Food is a great ice-breaker. Friends and guests simply love to maneuver around a table covered in great food to taste appetizers and to chat about relationships, sports, and travels.

Remember that there are no hard-and-fast rules. Almost anything goes at a tailgate, from sandwiches to stews and soups, which are among the easiest dishes to make.

A good policy is to balance your picnic foods. Offer foods that taste best cold with those that are great at any temperature. Crisp and crunchy foods like chips, crackers, and fresh vegetables work great with spreads and creamy dips.

Surprise your friends with something adventuresome and different each week. Bring something sweet at least every other game beause you can't miss with a dessert.

WINNING MENUS

Since everything tastes better outdoors, prepare early for rave reviews from friends and family at your next tailgate. Appetites are always better in exhilarating fall air. A little advance planning and preparation eliminates the need to rush around on Game Day and makes your picnic a stress-free success.

In this chapter, we've included 11 Game Day menus that bring together some of the best edibles in *Southern Tailgating*.

In the Southeast, temperatures outdoors can remain mild or warm (sometimes hot) well into September, but by October the air begins cooling all the way to bowl season. By mid-November, it can get as cold as a swamp frog's heart.

Early in the football season, spiced iced teas and fruit coolers make good warm-weather refreshers. As the temperature drops for mid-season games, ciders, coffee, and hot cocoas help warm any soul.

It's fun to plan a tailgate picnic. Your foods can be simple or or you can go all out. Rarely do you need to bring more than four foods, although the more you take the better. Your friends at your tailgate will bring something too, and there will be plenty to eat.

TAILGATERS ALLOWED

Local governments recognize the economic impact of tailgating. Officials in Athens-Clarke County, Georgia, in 1994, passed a strict ordinance forbidding glass containers or open containers of alcohol from public streets, sidewalks, and parking lots. The law as originally adopted was not applied to tailgating at University of Georgia home football games. However, no longer are football Saturdays exempted from the open-container ordinance. On the Georgia campus, though, officials say that the "University of Georgia is responsible for its jurisdiction."

GAME-BY-GAME MENUS

Your tailgating parties will be more fun when you plan different meals with different menus. Variety will add life. Be creative in planning each meal's dishes. You should use your own imagination to plan meals that appeal to your and your guests' particular tastes, but here are some suggested recipes for complete meals for the entire football season.

■ **September**

Game #1

Beverage:	Cranberry Apple Cooler
Appetizer:	Simply Great Deviled Eggs
Dip:	Cheese Dip
Main dish:	Bulldog Bites
Dessert:	Bulldog Swirl Brownies

TAILGATER GRIZZARD

The late columnist and humorist Lewis Grizzard was a Great American Tailgater. His third wife recalled how the couple rose early on each Game Day to pack a picnic of fried chicken, barbecue, and coolers of beer.

With radio and miniature television in tow, the couple arrived at Georgia's Sanford Stadium by 10 a.m. and spent the next four hours lunching with friends from the back of a car.

"All the way to the game, Lewis would recite to me the life history of every player and coach and then quiz me to make sure I was paying attention," wrote Kathy Grizzard Schmook.

Game #2

Beverage:	Opening Kickoff Tea
Appetizer:	Gater Bowl Creamy Fresh Fruit Dip; Roasted Pecans
Main dish:	Baked Parmesan Chicken
Dessert:	Pineapple Pound Cake

Game #3

Beverage:	Lime Tide; Iced Tea
Salad:	Sugar Bowl Bound Salad
Main dish:	Fire Up the Bulldogs Shrimp
Dessert:	Chocolate Bar Pie

Game #4

Beverage:	Cranberry Apple Cooler
Main dish:	Giant Cheeseburger on Giant Burger Bun, served with chips
Dessert:	Bulldog Peanut Butter Chocolate Swirl Fudge

■ **October**

Game #5

Beverage:	Orange Sangria
Appetizer:	Cream Cheese and Pineapple Spread or Dip

Salad: Tailgate Potato Salad
Main dish: Roast Arkansas Pork Barbecue
Dessert: Apple Cake

Game #6

Beverage: Apple Iced Tea
Appetizer: Dog Gone Puppy Chow
Main dish: Pile 'Em Up Sandwiches
Dessert: Nutty No Bake Cookies

Game #7

Beverage: Burgundy Apple Punch
Main dish: Louisiana Spaghetti Unlimited
Bread: Bread Sticks
Vegetable: Green Bean Casserole
Dessert: Chocolate Pound Cake Frosting ("Wonderful
             Fudge")

Game #8

Beverage: War Eagle Tea
Appetizer: Bulldog Salsa with chips
Main dish: Kentucky Wildcat Sandwich
Dessert: Jenny's Tiger Turtle Brownies

■ November

Game #9

Beverage: Yellow Jacket Citrus Fizz Punch
Salad: Bama "QB Keeper" Salad
Meat: Grecian Meatballs
Sandwich: Ham and Asparagus Roll Ups
Dessert: Auburn Orange Mini Cake

Game #10

Beverage: Crimson Cider; Coffee
Appetizer: Tomato and Bacon Spread
Soup: Beer Cheese Soup
Main dish: Ham & Swiss Cheese Sandwiches
Dessert: Roll Tide Gingerbread

Game #11

Beverage: Hot Cocoa for a Crowd; Tea
Main dish: Peter Rabbit Stew
Bread: Beer Bread
Dessert: Bulldog Nut Pastries

AUTUMN ORANGE

It's hard to beat an orange and gold autumn in Knoxville. More than 95,000 Tennessee fans stream into Neyland Stadium and its natural grass playing field, after breaking camps across campus.

Like great armies of old, these Volunteers set up mini-camps before the game using quilts and hammocks, folding tables and chairs, and ice boxes filled to the hilt.

The spreads at these annual fall reunions resemble a Hall-of-Fame for Mama's home cookin': fried chicken, deviled eggs, country ham sandwiches, potato salad, sun-brewed sweet tea, and homemade peach pies.

Radios are tuned to the pregame show. Somewhere in the crowd a man who hasn't missed a game in 31 years is playing a home-recorded cassette tape featuring Volunteer game highlights and Appalachian bluegrass music. Some fans read newspapers, and others play cards and tell jokes. Men and women alike talk about football, children, or religion, or simply rub their stomachs and muse about "how good all this here food is."

TIPS FOR SUCCESSFUL TAILGATING

NO NEED TO SHOW UP EMPTY-HANDED
25 THINGS YOU CAN GRAB ON THE WAY TO THE GAME

1. Grapes
2. Barbecue Pork
3. Mayonnaise
4. Bread
5. Pretzels
6. Mustard Dip
7. Apples
8. Caramel Dip

9. Chips
10. Dip
11. Soft Drinks
12. Peanuts
13. Pizza
14. Sub Sandwiches
15. Fried Chicken
16. Deli-Made Potato Salad
17. Deli-Made Dessert
18. Cookies
19. Crackers
20. Large bag of M&M's
21. Pepperidge Farm Gold Fish
23. Dill Pickles
24. Rolls
25. Red Lobster Shrimp Tray is great!

SERVING BUFFET

If you use a folding table, the buffet style works best. Move the table away from your car so that people can gather at each end and move around the table clockwise. People usually begin on the end of the table where paper or plastic plates are stacked.

Of course, a station wagon or Blazer-type folding tailgate creates an instant buffet table.

A folding director's chair is easy to transport and requires less space than a lawn chair.

COOLERS

Coolers filled with ice can be stored in your car during the game. Food that can be stored in plastic containers is the easiest to transport.

Your cooler can rest in an open trunk. The ice can double for drinks and for keeping things cold. Also, water frozen in two-liter bottles or other "bottled or canned" ice works great in keeping food from spoiling.

BEVERAGES

Always bring a non-alcoholic beverage, even if you are certain others at your tailgate will do the same. Beverages are consumed the fastest. There can never be too many soft drinks or tea, especially on hot Game Days.

PORTABLE FOODS

If you travel more than two hours, you'll prefer foods that don't fall apart or run together or get cold if they are supposed to stay warm. Think portable. Select foods that can be stored in paper sacks and plastic baggies.

If you keep foods wrapped and frozen until the morning of the game, especially if you travel to the game, you can use them to keep other foods cold. They'll be thawed and ready to eat by the picnic.

TAKING CHILDREN TO THE GAME

If you bring young children to the game, pack small toys and candy or snacks to take inside the stadium. Foam footballs, Frisbees, and headsets with cassettes help keep youngsters occupied if adult chatter starts to bore them.

Special treats like M&M's are good emergency awards for preschoolers or comfort for little tears. Grapes offer a healthy and non-messy snack for traveling to the game.

Once inside the stadium, kids respond well to lots of little toys and books to "read."

CHECKLIST OF ITEMS TO TAKE WITH YOU
FOR A PERFECT GAME DAY

Picnic basket
Cooler with ice
Tablecloth (cloth or plastic)
Flatware, plates, glasses (plastic or paper)
Folding table (if needed)
Folding chairs
Bottle opener
Large Thermos for hot drinks (and a second for hotdogs, if desired)
Sharp knife, spatula, large plastic spoon
Nutcracker
Paper towels and napkins

Matches
Platter or cutting board
Grill and charcoal, if necessary
Water spritzer (Keep near grill to extinguish the flames.)
Sterno or canned heat, if necessary
Insect repellent (Yellow jackets love picnics.)
Small first-aid kit
Umbrella (for tailgate) and raincoat or plastic slip-over (for stadium)
Large plastic garbage bag
Extra leakproof container
Stadium seat/cushion
Radio headset
Sunglasses
Binoculars
Sunblock or sun screen
Instant camera, for kids to take candid shots and for adults to use
Pocket money
Cinnamon sticks or ground cinammon (discourages ants if spread around legs of folding table or at edges of blanket or tablecloth)

STORIES

One of the best parts of tailgating is sharing stories with friends. Here are some to add to your trivia or store in your repertoire—or simply to read for the fun of it!

PROVE THEM WRONG

The Depression years were hard on most Americans, including young Paul "Bear" Bryant. His father died, and his mother remained in Fordyce, Arkansas, to scratch out a living.

During those years, Bryant was recruited to play football at Alabama. He became a starter.

He became discouraged during his sophomore years. He wrote an Arkansas cousin that he planned to quit the football team and get a job in a Texas oil field.

Bryant's cousin telegraphed him almost immediately. "GO

AHEAD AND QUIT, JUST LIKE EVERYONE PREDICTED
YOU WOULD."

The message changed Bryant's life. He refused to quit the
team. He eventually won more games than any other head
coach in Division I college football history.

Bryant later said that courage means sticking things out
with enthusiasm when times get tough.

THE TAIL GATORS

Not all tailgaters arrive at ballgames early and stuff
themselves with food. Some arrive early at nightclubs to warm
up.

The Tail Gators, a retro blues-rock band, earned a reputa-
tion for infectious guitar instrumentals and a rockabilly spirit.
"We'll have a real good time," the trio sings on their "Hide
Your Eyes" album.

PASS HAPPY

Coach Bobby Bowden, the respected pass master at Florida
State, preferred the running game during his tenure at West
Virginia. Georgia's Vince Dooley, known for his run-dominated
offenses, explained that Bowden turned to the passing game
when he got to FSU because the weather favored it and the
wide-open play would sell tickets and attract players.

AN OLYMPIC VISION

Porter led a demanding life as a young lineman on Georgia
Coach Wallace Butts' football team in the late 1940s.

He and his wife Mary, who married at 16, had a daughter
before Porter ever played one down as a Bulldog. Since housing
was scarce after World War II, the young family lived in an
Athens hotel for six months.

During Porter's sophomore year, a son, Billy, was born at an
Athens hospital. Georgia assistant coach Ralph "Shug" Jordan,
who later coached at Auburn, also had a son born at that same
hospital that day. Ralph and Porter flew to Oklahoma that
morning for a game.

Other Georgia players would help babysit Porter and
Mary's children. Mary thanked them with homemade ice

cream.

While in his early 20s, Porter became the youngest man to officiate games in the Southeastern Conference. His son Billy grew up to be a top receiver at Georgia under Coach Vince Dooley. Between them, Porter and Billy played on four SEC championship teams.

Billy became a lawyer, but like his Dad, remained closed to sports and athletics. In fact, it was Billy *Payne*, Porter and Mary's son, who shared with the world an Olympic vision for Georgia and Atlanta, and became head of the Atlanta Committee for the Centennial Olympic Games.

ONLY ERK

Erk Russell, a beloved defensive coordinator at Georgia from 1964-80 who later coached Georgia Southern to national titles, tried to describe how he felt after Georgia beat Notre Dame for the 1980 national championship.

"To be there at the end of the game and to know your team was going to be named national champion was an experience nobody would ever forget," Russell said.

The crush of celebrating Georgia fans who stormed the floor of New Orleans's Super Dome that night caught him unprepared.

"You know, what I had visualized, was that we could get our team out in the middle of the field and just sit there and all of us smoke a good cigar and soak it in," Russell told an interviewer. "But as you know, the crowd was on the field from the moment the game was over, and everybody had to run for their life just to get away from that crazy crowd."

PRACTICAL JOKE

Prior to the 1961 game with LSU, Mississippi players received a package, postmarked in Louisiana, filled with a large assortment of panties.

PUT COACH IN

Wallace Butts, who coached at Georgia during the 1940s and '50s, was infamous for fiery locker room lectures on team errors and pride.

After one chilling halftime talk, one Georgia player told an assistant coach, "When we get inside their 20-yard-line, put Coach Butts in; he's ready."

ROAD TRIP

Florida's first victory over a major out-of-state college occurred on Oct. 19, 1922. The Gators beat South Carolina's Gamecocks.

THE ROSE ELEPHANTS

The University of Alabama's elephant mascot can be traced back to the 1926 Rose Bowl between Alabama and the University of Washington. The owner of a Birmingham trunk company gave each team member a large piece of luggage emblazoned with his company's symbol—a red elephant standing atop a suitcase. Reporters immediately noticed the suitcases and their symbol as the players disembarked from their train. Subsequently, in game stories, they began to compare the winning Tide team to a powerful herd of elephants.

Another story says that Alabama's elephant mascot originated during the team's 1930 National Championship season. In describing third-quarter play in a clash with Ole Miss, *Atlanta Journal* sports writer Everett Strupper wrote that "the earth began to tremble, there was a distant rumble that continued to grow. Some excited fan in the stands bellowed, `Hold your horses, the elephants are coming,' and out stamped the Alabama varsity."

Strupper and other writers continued to refer to the Alabama linemen, who wore red jerseys, as "Red Elephants."

SANDS OF VICTORY

Not even World War II or North Africa's Sahara Desert could stop LSU and Tulane from staging an annual football classic on Thanksgiving Day, 1943.

Players were recruited from the LSU and Tulane Army Medical Units stationed near Bizerte, Tunisia, where the grudge match was played.

A makeshift, dusty field, crudely marked with various objects, was created from a patch of desert about the size of a football field. Tulane was the designated home team, but Tunisia was a long way from uptown New Orleans.

After the game, won by Tulane's passing game, players from both schools gathered at a small officers' bar set up at a nearby barrack. At the post-game "tailgate" party, revelers sipped eau de vie, a cognac created by pressing a grapevine's stems, twigs, and leaves.

"It was cheap and it was terrible," recalled Tulane player, Dr. Edward Mathews.

SATURDAY NIGHT LIGHTS

Former athletic director T.P. "Skipper" Heard introduced LSU's tradition of playing night games in 1931. Why play at night? The afternoon games were too hot and humid in southern Louisiana. Night games also allowed some fans who were busy tending plantations on Saturday afternoons a chance to watch the Tigers play. The tradition has continued ever since.

BOWL TICKETS—PLEASE!

Shortly after Florida State assistant coach Brad Scott was named head coach at South Carolina, he commented on the high expectations of Gamecock fans.

"I saw a bunch of our fans recently and they were all excited. They said, 'Hey coach, we're going to the Sugar Bowl!'" Scott recalled. "I told them that was great and would they please get me some tickets because I wanted to go too."

SKINNED ONLY ONCE

When Pat Dye—who resigned under pressure during the highly-publicized Eric Ramsey play-for-pay investigation—was head coach at Auburn, he said that despite some bad publicity, he got "a kick out of the press."

But if a sportswriter wrote something Dye felt was dishonest, the coach might say so. He might even get even with that sports writer in future interviews by giving dull, "vanilla" answers.

Dye described his relationship with reporters as such: "You can clip a sheep every year, but you don't skin him but once."

SEMINOLES BEAT STATESMEN

When Florida State University played its first football game on October 18, 1947, the team didn't have a nickname. Immediately, students rallied together and submitted several potential nicknames to be voted on by the entire student body. A week after the first game, the list was narrowed to six names: Golden Falcons, Statesmen, Crackers, Senators, Indians, and Seminoles. The moniker Seminoles eventually beat out Statesmen by 110 votes.

SWITCHAROO

In 1980, Auburn's football team tried to psyche out Georgia's players by warming up in traditional blue jerseys, but coming out for the opening kickoff in orange jerseys. The ploy failed to work. Georgia won, 31-20, en route to an undefeated season and a national championship.

TARKENTON'S DEFENSE

Georgia's final home game against Georgia Tech in 1960 was the final game for seniors and Bulldog standouts Fran Tarkenton and Pat Dye.

It also turned out to be final game for legendary Bulldog head coach Wallace Butts. Tarkenton, the All-Southeastern Conference quarterback who later made the NFL Hall of Fame, saved the Tech game with a few seconds to play.

Georgia Tech quarterback Stan Gan hurled a pass down field. Tarkenton, then playing free safety, intercepted Gann's pass and ran down the sideline in front of coach Butts.

Instead of staying in bounds and running out the clock, Tarkenton ran out of bounds with seconds remaining.

"[EXPLETIVE], Francis, you've been here four years and you ain't made contact yet!," Butts screamed as he leapt into the air.

Georgia won anyway, 7-6, thanks largely to Dye. The future Auburn head coach blocked a field goal and an extra point during the game.

The Bulldogs never lost to arch-rival Tech during the four years Tarkenton and Dye played at Georgia.

NO TEETH ARE NO EXCUSE

Charles "Sid" Belflower, an Athens hospital security guard who once served as Vince Dooley's personal aide, recalls a favorite story about Heyward Allen, a captain and tailback on Coach Wally Butts' 1941 Bulldog team.

The Dogs were playing hated rival Florida in the old Gator Bowl in Jacksonville.

"Some big lineman tackled Allen and hit him in the mouth, knocking out two of Allen's front teeth," said Belflower. "Allen drops to his knees and starts looking for his teeth in the grass. He finally looks up and calls time out, but continues to comb the floor of the Gator Bowl looking for his teeth.

"'Allen, what in the hell are you doing?'" screamed a bewildered Coach Butts, a small but fiery man whose famous temper could tame a wild boar.

"Allen, whose mouth was bleeding profusely, explained that he was looking for his teeth.

"'[Expletive] your teeth,'" yelled Butts. "'Get in the game! We're playing Florida!'"

THE LONGEST PUNT

On an exceptionally windy day in Annapolis, Maryland, in 1925, Marquette quarterback Bob Demoling took a snap at his team's own 25 yard line and punted the ball to the Navy 19.

The ball bounced and was carried by the gusting wind across the end zone and 30 yards into Chesapeake Bay, where it was swept out to sea.

Officials never determined total yardage, but Marquette claims the longest punt ever.

THE CHAMPS

Alabama has appeared in more national bowl games than any other college. Coach Wallace Wade led his teams to national football championships in 1925 and 1926. The University won national championships in 1961, 1964, 1965, 1973, 1978, and 1979, all under its legendary coach Paul "Bear" Bryant. Alabama won the 1992 national championship under Coach Gene Stallings, a former assistant under Bryant. Alabama ranks only behind Notre Dame and Oklahoma for most national championships (according to AP rankings).

TOTAL HUMILIATION

Georgia Tech demolished little Cumberland College of Lebanon, Tennessee, 222-0 in Atlanta on October 7, 1916—the most lopsided game in college football history.

Not all was lost for the out-matched Bulldogs. Cumberland's football manager, George Allen, who collected Cumberland's guaranteed $500 payment, later advised several American presidents as director of the U.S. Reconstruction Finance Corp.

TENNESSEE ORANGE

Charles Moore, a member of the first football team in 1891, selected the school colors of orange and white. Approved by a school vote, the colors were those of the common American daisy which was native to the area. Tennessee players did not appear in their orange jerseys until the season opening game in 1922. Legend says that the uniforms may have been instrumental in helping the team defeat Emory and Henry by a score of 50-0.

THEY LIVE AT THE STADIUM

LSU's stadium, widely known as Death Valley, once housed some 1,500 dorm rooms. When Coach Skipper Heard learned that LSU president James Smith was planning to spend $250,000 on new campus dormitories, Heard had an idea.

Heard convinced Smith to raise the stands on both the east and west sides and expand them to the end zones. It proved to be a win-win compromise. The dorms were built inside Tiger Stadium, which satisfied Smith, and the stadium grew by 10,000 seats.

VOLUN-FEAR

"Fan" is short for fanatic, and some football fans are known to get downright fanatic about their teams.

During the October 24, 1908, Tennessee-Georgia game in Knoxville, Georgia coach Steadman Sanford was frequently taunted and ridiculed on the sidelines by a group of Volunteer fans, some of them smelling of whiskey.

Midway through the first half, Georgia threatened to score first after reaching Tennessee's 2-yard line. A mountaineer sporting a frock coat and a wide-brimmed hat walked onto the field toward the Georgia huddle brandishing a .38 revolver.

"The first man who crosses that line," he warned, pointing his pistol toward the goal line, "will get a bullet in his carcass."

Police hustled the fanatic off the field, but the Georgia players never recovered their composure. The Bulldogs fumbled the ball to Tennessee on the next play and eventually lost 10-0.

WANNABE BOWLS

Dozens of college football bowl games have come and gone over the past 60 years. A fortunate few, like the Sugar, Orange, and Rose, have maintained prestige and grown into annual classics. The bowls that faltered include New York's Gotham Bowl (1961-62), the 1931 Bacardi Bowl in Havana, Cuba, and Los Angeles' one-time Mercy Bowl in 1961.

WAR EAGLE

Auburn's famous battle cry, "War Eagle," is often confused for the school's nickname, the Tigers. The Tiger nickname comes from a line in English poet Oliver Goldsmith's poem, "The Deserted Village," published in 1770, "where crouching tigers wait their helpless prey...."

The name of the city and university originated from the same Goldsmith poem, which notes "Sweet Auburn, loveliest village of the plain...." Early sportswriters called Auburn athletes "Plainsmen."

Why the confusion over nicknames? One reason may be that War Eagle VI, Auburn's golden eagle mascot, is named Tiger!

WELCOME SOUTH, BULLDOGS!

Georgia whipped Yale, a national powerhouse in the 1920s, in the first game played in Sanford Stadium, which cost $360,000 to build on a natural amphitheater surrounding old Tanyard Creek.

The game was the Yale Bulldogs' first trip to the South.

The festival-type atmosphere surrounding that October 1929 weekend and the historic dedication game drew 27 train loads of visitors and 60 airplanes to Athens. A national audience tuned to the game on radio.

One Southern sports historian noted after Georgia's 15-0 shutout that the game was "the biggest thing to happen in the South since Appomattox—except we won."

THEM D-A-AWGS

"HOW 'BOUT THEM D-A-AWGS?" barks the Rev. John Brown, a Methodist pastor from Sparta, Georgia. Brown is likely to verbalize his support anywhere his beloved Bulldogs play. And, regardless of where he is on a Saturday night, the avid tailgater is always back behind his middle Georgia pulpit by Sunday morning.

🍴

NOTES

Index

ALL-STAR WEST-OF-THE-BORDER DIP 35
APPLE CAKE 136
APPLE CRUMB PIE 138
APPLE DELIGHT 136
APPLE ICED TEA 5
AUBURN MISTAKES 102
AUBURN ORANGE MINI CAKES 137
AUBURN TIGER STEW 86

BAKED PARMESAN CHICKEN 107
BAMA "QB KEEPER" SALAD 72
BARBECUE CUPS 104
BEER BREAD 39
BEER CHEESE SOUP 79
BIG AL COCOA PEANUT LOGS 125
BLAIR'S TOASTED PECANS 24
BLUEBERRY CREAM PIE 139
BOWERS BOYS' SPECIAL 54
BOWKNOTS 22
BREAD STICKS 45
BROCCOLI BREAD 39
BRUNSWICK STEW 88
BUFFALO WINGS 108
BULLDOG BITES 52
BULLDOG NUT PASTRIES 24
BULLDOG PEANUT BUTTER
CHOCOLATE SWIRL FUDGE 130
BULLDOG RED SAUCE FOR ROAST 93
BULLY'S BARBEQUE SAUCE 94
BURGUNDY APPLE PUNCH 10
BUSH WACKER 9

CALL THE HOGS SPINACH DIP 34
CARAMEL COOKIES 119
CHEESE BISCUITS 40
CHEESE DIP 36
CHEESE GRITS 115
CHEESECAKE BARS 128
CHEESY BEEF DIP 36
CHEESY CHICKEN 108
CHERRY TOMATO MEATBALLS 98
CHESS SQUARES 129
CHICKEN BALLS FOR AUBURN OR
CLEMSON 110
CHICKEN FLORENTINE QUICHE 111
CHICKEN IN A BISCUIT 56
CHICKEN SALAD 63
CHICKEN SALAD WITH GRAPES 64
CHOCOLATE BAR PIE 140
CHOCOLATE POUND CAKE
FROSTING 133
CLAUDETTE'S "DAWG RICH" PIE 140
COLD CONFETTI MEATLOAF 96
CORN SALAD 73
CRANBERRY APPLE COOLER 8
CRAWFISH ETOUFFEE 107

CREAM CHEESE AND PINEAPPLE
SPREAD OR DIP 31
CRIMSON CIDER 12
CROCKPOT SANDWICHES 58
CRUNCHY CHEESE WAFERS 21
CRUSTED PEANUTS 24
CURRY CHICKEN 111
CURRY COATED POPCORN 16

DAWG BITES 19
DICKSON STREET BANANA NUT
BREAD 42
DINNER ROLLS 43
DOG-GONE PUPPY CHOW 25
DOGGIE BURGERS 97

EGG ROLL TIDES 112
EVERY BULLDOG'S FAVORITE
CHOCOLATE CHIP COOKIE 125

FIESTA BUTTERED POPCORN 26
FIRE UP TO WIN SHRIMP 106
FOOTBALL PIMENTO CHEESE 51
FRESH GARDEN GAZPACHO SOUP 80
FRIED STEAK 104

GATOR BOWL CREAMY FRESH FRUIT
DIP 33
GEORGIA SWEET AND SOUR AUBURN
PINEAPPLE MEATBALLS 100
GIANT BURGER BUN 43
GIANT CHEESEBURGER 44
GOAL LINE CHEESE STRAWS 20
GOAL POST GOODIES 17
GRANDMOTHER'S COOKIES 124
GRANOLA 26
GRECIAN MEATBALLS 101
GREEN AND GOLD BUTTERED
POPCORN 16
GREEN BEAN CASSEROLE 114
GRILL'EM AT THE STADIUM STEAKS 94
GUACAMOLE DIP 38
GUMBO BURGERS 57

HAM AND ASPARAGUS ROLLUPS 58
HAM AND CHEESE TREATS 45
HAM AND SWISS CHEESE
SANDWICHES 52
HAM SPREAD 33
HIDDEN VALLEY RANCH
QUESADILLAS 23
HOMEMADE MACARONI AND
CHEESE 113
HOT COCOA FOR A CROWD 11
HUNGRY DAWG CHOWDER 89

ICEBOX FRUITCAKE 137
INCREDIBLE TIDE EDIBLES 131
JENNY'S TIGER TURTLE BROWNIES 134
KENTUCKY WILDCAT SANDWICH 53
LEMON-BASIL BUTTERED POPCORN 16
LIME TIDE 9
LOUISIANA SPAGHETTI UNLIMITED 110
MARINATED SHRIMP AND PASTA
  SALAD 64
MARY LOU'S SPECIAL 10
MARZIPANS 133
MEXICAN CORN BREAD 40
MEXICAN ROLLUPS 59
MEXICAN SALAD 65
MINCEMEAT SQUARES 134
MINI CHEESECAKES 135
MISSISSIPPI PUPPY CHOW 25
MSU ALUMNI ANTIPASTA 68
MSU MINT BROWNIES 127

N0. 1 FINGER SALAD 73
NO BAKE OATMEAL COOKIES 120
NUT PARTY MIX 21
NUTTY NO BAKE COOKIES 120
OLÉ DIP 37
OOEGG 135
OPENING KICKOFF ICED TEA 5
ORANGE SANGRIA 11
OZARK AUTUMN SPICED TEA 15

PARMESAN POPCORN 16
PARTY WINGS CHILI 18
PEACH CANDY 132
PECAN ICE CREAM SUNDAE SAUCE 140
PEPPER MEDLEY 68
PETER RABBIT STEW 80
PIG SOOEY CORN CHEX TREATS 26
PILE 'EM UP SANDWICHES 56
PIMENTO CHEESE SPREAD 51
PINEAPPLE POUND CAKE 138
PIZZA DIP 38
POLYNESIAN MEATBALLS 102

POPCORN POTPOURRI 16
PRALINES 132

QUICK TRIFLE 138

RAISIN BRAN MUFFINS 41
RAZORBACK SAUSAGE HOAGIES 57
REBEL SALSA 34
ROAST ARKANSAS PORK BARBECUE 103
ROASTED PECANS 17
ROLL TIDE GINGERBREAD 130
RUSHING YARDS SPICE TEA 15

SAUSAGE BALLS 105
SAUSAGE CHEESE BALLS 105
SEC CHAMP STEW 87
SIMPLY GREAT DEVILED EGGS 23
SIX-LAYER HOG TREAT 121
SOUTH CAROLINA GAMECOCK SUB
  SANDWICH 54
SOUTHERN COMFORT DAWGS 19
SPAGHETTI SALAD 67
SPICY BEEF BRISKET AND SAUCE 109
STARS FELL OVER ALABAMA BLT
  SALAD 74
STEWED YELLOW JACKET 86
STRAWBERRY DIP 39
SUGAR BOWL BOUND SALAD 69
SWEET AND SOUR SAUSAGES 106
SWIRL BROWNIES 126

TAILGATE POTATO SALAD 71
TAILGATERS' MINIATURE REUBENS 20
TEXAS BEAN SALAD 72
TIGER DELIGHT CHICKEN 113
TOMATO AND BACON SPREAD 31

ULTIMATE BULLDOG CHOCOLATE
  CHIP COOKIE 122
VARSITY VEG-ALL 114
WAR EAGLE TEA 8
WONDERFUL FUDGE 133
YELLOW JACKET CITRUS FIZZ PUNCH 6

COLLEGE NICKNAMES
And Other Interesting Sports Traditions

Featuring stories from 342 schools across the nation—including all SEC and ACC schools—*College Nicknames* brings together anecdotes and informative facts in one convenient place.

"An enjoyable trip to 342 campuses for the stories behind their nicknames, mascots, and other interesting facts. Fascinating!"— *Scholastic Coach*

By Joanne Sloan and Cheryl Watts
1993. Softcover. 364 pages. 6 x 9. $13.95

ALABAMA TALES
Anecdotes, Legends, and Stories

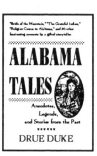

This entertaining collection tells of both the famous and little-known people and events that shaped Alabama. The Huntsville trial of the outlaw Frank James, the promise of George Washington Carver to become a teacher, the first wedding in America—these and other stories provide vivid glimpses into Alabama's past.

"The stories are concise, adventurous, and full of action....I read each story with anticipation and felt as though I was there when it happened.... This is a great book."— Jesse Joiner, retired principal

"Pithy, rooted in history and fascinating detail, rich with lore....If you want to do a friend or a young person a real favor, read one aloud and you'll both have a great time."— James McDermott, Senior Editor, *Guideposts*

By Drue Duke
1994. Softcover. 154 pages. 5 1/2 x 8 1/2 $9.95

DISCONNECTED
Public Opinion and Politics in Alabama

Why doesn't Alabama politics work? The authors, experts in Alabama public opinion, present lively and provocative answers. The analysis is based on Southern Opinion Research polls they have conducted over the last five years. Well-written and handsomely illustrated, the book will fascinate anyone interested in Alabama politics, the state's news media, or the public's attitudes.

By P. Cotter, J. Stovall, & S. Fisher
1994. Softcover. 200 pp. 6 x 9. $14.95

ORDER FORM

Books from Vision Press make entertaining and informative reading for you and your family, and they are ideal as gifts for friends.

To order a book, please complete this form and mail it to:
Vision Press
P.O. Box 1106
Northport, AL 35476

Please enclose your check payable to Vision Press.

Please send me the following book(s):

QTY	TITLE	PRICE	TOTAL
____	*Southern Tailgating*	$12.95	____
____	*Alabama Tales*	$9.95	____
____	*College Nicknames*	$13.95	____
____	*Disconnected: Public Opinion*	$14.95	____

Alabama residents, please add 4% sales tax: ____

Handling and postage: $1.50 per book: ____

TOTAL: _____

Name:

Address:

City, State, Zip:

Please send the following book(s), along with a card to the recipient acknowledging the books as a gift from me, to:

Name:

Address:

City, State, Zip:

QTY	TITLE	PRICE	TOTAL
____	*Southern Tailgating*	$12.95	____
____	*Alabama Tales*	$9.95	____
____	*College Nicknames*	$13.95	____
____	*Disconnected: Public Opinion*	$14.95	____

Alabama residents, please add 4% sales tax: ____

Handling and postage: $1.50 per book: ____

TOTAL: _____